THEMATIC UNIT
Ancient India

Written by Michelle Breyer, M.A.

Illustrated by Bruce Hedges
Cover Art by Larry Bauer
Edited by Barbara M. Wally, M.S.

Teacher Created Materials, Inc.

6421 Industry Way

Westminster, CA 92683

©1998 Teacher Created Materials, Inc.

Made in U.S.A.

ISBN 1-55734-577-5

The classroom teacher may reproduce copies of materials in this book for classroom use only. The reproduction of any part for an entire school or school system is strictly prohibited. No part of this publication may be transmitted, stored, or recorded in any form without written permission from the publisher.

Table of Contents

Introduction

Ancient India contains a comprehensive whole language, thematic unit. Its 80 reproducible pages are filled with a wide variety of lesson ideas designed for use with intermediate and middle school students. At its core are two high-quality reading selections: *Exploration Into India* and *Tusk and Stone*.

For each of these books, activities are included which set the stage for reading, encourage enjoyment of the book, and extend the concepts presented. Additional activities that integrate the theme into curriculum areas of language arts (including writing and research skills), math, science, social studies, art, music, and life skills are also provided. Many of these activities are conducive to the use of cooperative learning groups. Most of these activities may be used with either selection, should you choose to use only one of the books.

Suggestions and patterns for bulletin boards and unit management tools are additional time savers for the busy teacher. Directions for culminating activities such as the ABC Picture Book of India, Caste System Dramas, and an Indian Living History Day, allow students to synthesize their knowledge in order to create products that can be shared beyond the classroom.

This thematic includes the following:

- ❑ **literature selections**—summaries of two books with related lessons that cross the curriculum

- ❑ **fine arts**—suggestions for activities in music, drama, poetry, and the visual arts

- ❑ **planning guides**—suggestions for sequencing lessons of the unit

- ❑ **writing ideas**—suggestions for a variety of writing activities that cross the curriculum

- ❑ **bulletin boards**—suggestions and plans for content-related and interactive bulletin boards

- ❑ **home/school connections**—ideas for extending learning into the student's home

- ❑ **curriculum connections**—activities in language arts, math, science, social studies, fine arts, and life skills

- ❑ **group projects**—activities to foster cooperative learning

- ❑ **technology**—examples of videos and computer programs to enhance the student's learning

- ❑ **culminating activities**—projects which require students to synthesize their learning and participate in activities that can be shared with others

- ❑ **bibliography**—a suggested list of additional literature, non-fiction books, software and Internet resources relating to this unit

Introduction *(cont.)*

Why a Balanced Approach?

The strength of a balanced language approach is that it involves children in using all modes of communication—reading, writing, listening, illustrating, and speaking. Communication skills are interconnected and integrated into lessons which emphasize the whole of language rather than isolating its parts. Balancing this approach is our knowledge that every whole—including individual words—is composed of parts, and the directed study of those parts can help a student to master the whole. Experience and research tell us that regular attention to phonics, other word attack skills, spelling, etc., develops reading mastery, thereby completing the unity of the whole language experience. The child reads, writes (spelling appropriately for his or her level), speaks, listens, and thinks in response to a literature experience introduced by the teacher. In these ways language skills grow rapidly, stimulated by involvement and interest in the topic at hand.

Why Thematic Planning?

One very useful tool for implementing an integrated whole language program is thematic planning. By choosing a theme with correlating selections for a unit of study, a teacher can plan activities throughout the day that lead to a cohesive, in-depth study of the topic. Students will be practicing and applying their skills in meaningful contexts. Consequently, they will tend to learn and retain more. Both teachers and students will be freed from a day that is broken into unrelated segments of isolated drill and practice.

Why Cooperative Learning?

In addition to academic skills and content, students need to learn social skills. No longer can this area of development be taken for granted. Students must learn to work cooperatively in groups in order to function well in modern society. Group activities should be a regular part of school life, and teachers should consciously include social objectives as well as academic objectives in their planning. The teacher should clarify and monitor the qualities of good leader-follower group interaction, just as he or she would clarify and monitor the academic goals of the project.

Why Technology?

Our students are rapidly approaching the real world where knowledge of technological advances is a must. In order for our students to compete outside the classroom, it is necessary for them to have a wide range of technological experiences including an understanding of word processing, multi-media presentations, video, and computer simulations. Technology also helps motivate students and enhance their learning experience by providing another avenue to gain and report information.

Exploration Into India

by Anita Ganeri

Summary

This non-fiction book explores the history of India from ancient times to the modern day. The book is divided into six chapters describing the eras of Indian history in chronological order. Beginning with the Indus Valley civilization and the arrival of the Aryans with their caste system, this book introduces students to the invaders and traders who explored the vast subcontinent. Each new group of visitors added to the culture of the country, some with religion and philosophy, others with language, and still others with unique styles of art and architecture.

This outline is a suggested plan for using the various activities that are presented in this book. Each of the lessons can take from one to several days to complete.

Sample Plan

Lesson 1

- ❏ Complete one or more of the Setting the Stage activities, page 6.
- ❏ Read pages 4–7 of *Exploration Into India*.
- ❏ Create a map of India, page 51.
- ❏ Introduce the Indian vocabulary lists, page 41.
- ❏ Design an Ancient Indian City, page 61.
- ❏ Make an Indus Valley Seal Print, page 66.
- ❏ Read and discuss The Indus Valley Civilization, pages 52–54.

Lesson 2

- ❏ Read pages 8–11 of the book.
- ❏ Continue defining Indian vocabulary.
- ❏ Make A Classroom *Rig-Veda*, page 42.
- ❏ Research the Hindu Gods and complete the activity on pages 56–58.
- ❏ Complete Indian Caste System Questions and Activities, page 9.
- ❏ Begin a Time Line of India, page 62.

Lesson 3

- ❏ Read pages 12 and 13 of the book.
- ❏ Continue defining Indian vocabulary.
- ❏ Read about and discuss The Legend of Buddha, pages 10-12.
- ❏ Complete activities on the Basic Beliefs of Buddhism, page 13.
- ❏ Discuss and complete Asoka's Edicts, page 15.
- ❏ Continue creating the Time Line of India, page 62.

Lesson 4

- ❏ Read pages 14 and 15 of the book.
- ❏ Continue defining Indian Vocabulary.
- ❏ Read about Kalidasa and write a poem, pages 16–17.
- ❏ Make a sculpture or cave painting, page 68.
- ❏ Compute Hindu-Arabic numbers, page 48.
- ❏ Continue creating the Time Line of India, page 62.

Lesson 5

- ❏ Read pages 16–19 of the book.
- ❏ Continue defining Indian Vocabulary.
- ❏ Make a Trade Route Map, page 60.
- ❏ Read and discuss Islam in India, page 18.
- ❏ Continue creating the Time Line of India, page 62.

Lesson 6

- ❏ Read Chapter 3 of *Exploration Into India*.
- ❏ Continue defining Indian Vocabulary.
- ❏ Compare the Mogul Emperors, page 19.
- ❏ Make a Taj Mahal, page 69.
- ❏ Continue creating the Time Line of India, page 62.

Lesson 7

- ❏ Read Chapter 4 of the book.
- ❏ Continue defining Indian Vocabulary.
- ❏ Learn about European visitors to India, page 20.
- ❏ Discuss the Jains and Sikhs in India, page 21.
- ❏ Compare India's main religions, page 59.
- ❏ Continue creating the Time Line of India, page 62.

Lesson 8

- ❏ Read Chapters 5 and 6 of the book.
- ❏ Complete the Indian Vocabulary.
- ❏ Describe the Life of a Maharajah, page 46.
- ❏ Write A Letter Home to England, page 22.
- ❏ Discuss India's struggle for independence, page 23.
- ❏ Learn to tie-dye, page 65.
- ❏ Complete the Time Line of India, page 62.
- ❏ Complete one or more culminating activities, pages 70–77.

Overview of Activities

Setting the Stage

1. Assemble the Ancient India Bulletin Board (page 78) for students to complete as the unit progresses.

2. Create folders to keep all notes and handouts organized for reference throughout the unit.

3. Have students brainstorm what they already know about India—food, animals, religions, geography, dress, language, etc. Write these ideas on the board. Introduce students to the land and people of India by reviewing their social studies texts, encyclopedias, and other resource materials on India. Encourage them to add details to the list.

4. Play some Indian music. Look for tapes or CDs by sitarist Ravi Shankar, especially *Sounds of India*. You may wish to explain to the students that Shankar influenced the Beatles and that many people explored Indian culture and philosophy as part of the "Hippie" era.

5. Introduce *Exploration Into India* and allow the students to look through the pictures to get an overview of the people they will be studying. Have students note that India is a melting pot, and many different people, religions, and cultures have shaped the nation.

Enjoying the Book

1. Read pages 4-7 of *Exploration Into India*. Discuss the geography of India and how life is shaped by the seasons of monsoons.

2. Have students make a map of India (page 51) to refer to throughout the unit.

3. Copy and distribute the vocabulary lists on page 41. Throughout the unit, assign appropriate words that appear in the pages or relate to the pages you are covering at the time. Students may want to note the page numbers where they found each vocabulary word, as well as defining the words. Encourage students to add other words from their reading to the appropriate categories.

4. Begin the history of India with the Indus Valley Civilization. Complete related lessons and activities as mentioned in the Sample Plan.

5. In small groups, or as a class, begin a Time Line of India (page 62). To help students understand the scope of India's history, you may wish to add events from other cultures to the time line(s) in groups or as a class. See page 46 of *Exploration Into India* and/or other reference materials.

Extending the Book

1. Review the history and people of India by creating an ABC Picture Book of India (page 70).

2. Have the students prepare Caste System Dramas (page 71).

3. Plan an Indian Living History Day to celebrate the wonders of India (page 72).

4. Read more about India and the many different people who call it home. See the Bibliography on page 79 for suggested resources. Have students read some Indian mythology and then write their own using the activity on page 44.

5. Ask students to describe what they find most fascinating about India and what they find most difficult to understand. What have the people of India brought to our country? How can we appreciate India in our daily lives?

The Indian Caste System

When the *Aryans* first migrated into the Indus Valley, they brought with them a culture which was totally different from any other in the region. The Aryans, who were nomads, did not dominate the land by building great cities out of stone and brick but instead left their mark in numerous other ways.

They passed on their Sanskrit language, which was used to compose formalized poetry such as the sacred *Rig-Veda* and other stories that drive home the universal values of righteous living. Although they could not write Sanskrit in the beginning, the oral language had a rich and thorough vocabulary. For example, in Sanskrit, the word *arya* means noble. The Aryans also contributed their religion which was based on set rituals that filtered into the daily lives of the inhabitants. Their military techniques and weapons were also far superior to others in the Middle East. The Aryans brought domesticated horses, the wheel, the chariot, and bronze weapons to Indian culture.

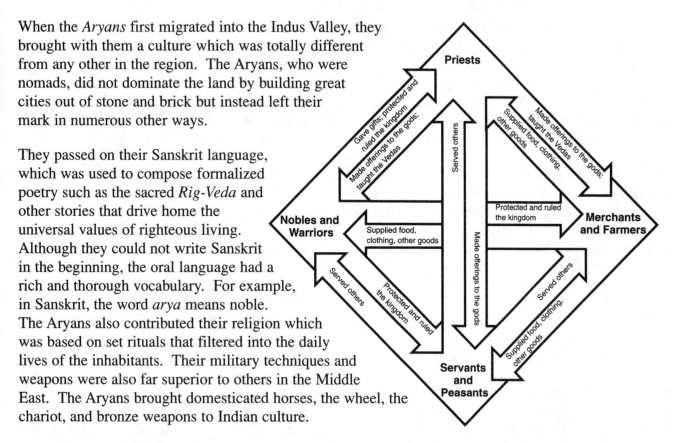

One of the most prominent contributions of the Aryans was their unique social structure. In their system every class had a duty in society to fulfill. This concept of divine moral duty was called *dharma*. Each class contributed to the others and received something in return. Originally there were three main classes or *varnas*. Because daily life was governed by religion and its rituals, the priests and scholars became the highest class, called *Brahmans*. Next came the ruling class, the *Kshatriyas*, which included nobles and warriors. The third class, made up of commoners, was called *Vaisyas*. Eventually, a fourth class, the *Sudras*, emerged, made up of servants and peasants.

People who did not follow their religious practices were considered unacceptable by the Aryans. They were called untouchables or *Panchamas* and were totally shunned by society and forced to live "outside" the class system. These people lived outside the villages and performed tasks considered too lowly for even the Sudras. They cleaned up after cremating the dead, executed criminals, tanned animal hides, and did other jobs seen as unclean. They were also supposed to eat from broken bowls and wear only clothes taken from the dead. As time passed, they were also forced to sound wooden clappers to warn people that they were coming because higher classes thought that they could be defiled by seeing an untouchable, or his or her shadow.

In the Aryan system, class was hereditary, and regardless of one's actions, he or she would remain in that class until death. There were very strict rules that governed the classes and dictated what they wore, what they ate, their occupations, their friends, whom they could marry, their duty, their destiny, and how they treated others. Although all classes had rights and were protected by law, the law varied depending upon one's class. For example, if a member of the highest or Brahman class hit and killed a servant, he would only have to pay a small fine. If a servant killed a priest, he would be executed.

The Indian Caste System *(cont.)*

By the medieval period there were divisions within the classes that were based on occupations or *jati*. These divisions were called *castes*. Like the classes, some castes were considered higher than others. One was born within a certain caste, worked within the caste, married within the caste, and one's children belonged to that caste. Although classes and castes are not the same, over time the two words have been merged together to include both groupings. Today there are about 3,000 different groups. Although it is now illegal to discriminate against the *Panchamas,* the caste system is still in effect throughout India. The main reason this class separation has persisted lies in the Hindu religion itself.

Three interlocking elements of belief are central to Hinduism. One of these beliefs is *samsara*, or reincarnation. Hindus believe that life is a ceaseless cycle of events with no beginning or end. Death and birth are both just phases of the cycle. Each person must live several lives, learning along the way, before achieving a final supreme goal of Absolute called *moksha*. Moksha is reached only when the individual has overcome all evils and all earthly desires. The soul can then be released, never to come back to Earth again.

This concept ties to *karma*, or the belief that everything a person does has a consequence. Both good and bad deeds have an effect on a person's happiness or misery in his or her present life, as well as in future lives. Whether one reappears in the next life as a plant, an insect, a *Brahman,* or a Panchama depends on actions performed in previous lives.

The third central element is the concept of *dharma*, or the belief that one should live according to his or her own moral duties appropriate to one's station in life. Because they believe in reincarnation and karma, Hindus feel that they should accept the level of life into which they are born and go about their daily routines and rituals within their caste without question or complaint. If they can do this well, then they will move up the caste ladder in their next life. The combination of these beliefs keeps the caste system strong in India. As long as the Hindu religion remains dominant in their culture, India will continue to uphold the caste system, regardless of the law.

Activity:

Divide the class into five groups. Decide on rules and privileges for each class, for instance, Brahmans go to lunch or recess first, etc. Assign a class to each group of students and follow the rules for a specified period of time, perhaps a day or several hours. Rotate so that each group has a chance to be each caste. When everyone has experienced each class, discuss how they felt, and what conclusions they can draw.

Caste System Questions and Activities

1. Use the chart below to compare the castes of India with our social classes. Work in small groups to fill in the types of people that would belong in each level for both societies. Discuss your findings as a class.

	Aryan India	**Our Society**
Highest Class		
Upper Class		
Middle Class		
Lower Class		
Outcast from Society		

2. Use the chart to discuss the following questions as a class: How did the Aryans determine one's class? What determines your class today? How did the Aryans distinguish the different people? How can we tell today to what class people belong? The Aryans could not change their class. Can you change yours? If so, how?

3. Do you feel that you are fulfilling a certain duty to society? What factors will determine your destiny?

4. The name *Aryan* means noble. How do you think the Aryans viewed themselves as they moved into the Indus Valley?

5. The term *Aryan* has become infamous this century because it was used by Hitler. How did Hitler use the term, and why is it regarded negatively now?

The Legend of Buddha

Many centuries ago in a peaceful kingdom in the foothills of the Himalaya mountains, there lived a king and queen who longed for a son to take the throne. One night the queen had a wonderful dream. A beautiful white elephant with six golden tusks came to her, gently touching her right side with a lotus flower. In the center of the lotus blossom glittered a brilliant jewel. Upon waking, she described the dream to her husband and the wise men of the kingdom. They all agreed that the dream foretold a miracle.

The wise men explained that a son would soon be born, a boy of great importance and promise. If the boy remained in the royal household, he would grow up to be a magnificent king and rule the world. However, if he ventured out, he would find the Truth and become a holy man set on becoming the savior of the world. This prophecy alarmed the king, for holy men at the time were poor beggars who wandered the land spreading their word. This was not a suitable future for his noble son, and he vowed to shelter the boy from life outside the kingdom walls.

Soon the prediction came true. One afternoon while the queen strolled through the royal gardens, the earth began to shake and quiver. The queen quickly grasped the branch of a nearby flowering tree as a baby boy emerged from her right side. Heavenly water rained down on the infant, bathing his head, and lotus blossoms fell from the skies. The boy was named Siddhartha, meaning "every wish fulfilled." There was great rejoicing in the palace, but the king was still disturbed by the prophecy. Adding to his sorrow, his beloved queen died seven days after the birth.

Siddhartha grew up surrounded by luxury and showered with love. The king ensured that the boy would never need or want anything or experience any pain. Only young, vibrant servants tended to his needs. The prince was sheltered from sickness and images of death. His father trained Siddhartha to become a great king. The young prince excelled in his lessons of language, math, science, and athletics and became an expert marksman and warrior. Despite all of these efforts the young prince was never carefree and often pondered the true meaning of life.

At the age of 16, Siddhartha married a beautiful princess. The king had three exquisite palaces built for the couple to ensure that Siddhartha would remain in the kingdom and fulfill his destiny as a great ruler. For 13 years Siddartha lived in the most splendid surroundings with a loving wife tending to his every need, but he still grew more and more restless. He yearned to see what lay beyond in the big world.

One day he commanded his chariot driver to carry him outside the kingdom. As they slipped beyond the palace gates, Siddhartha saw on the street an old man, a sick man, and a dead man. For the first time in his life, he witnessed human suffering.

"Does everyone became sick and old?" Siddhartha asked his driver, "Will everyone eventually die? What then? What becomes of us then?"

The Legend of Buddha *(cont.)*

The driver replied, "We all die." Siddhartha was filled with sorrow and disbelief. How could people laugh and sing knowing they would die? How can anyone live in peace knowing of all this suffering?

The next day Siddhartha, filled with curiosity, slipped away again. On this journey he met a monk in a saffron robe who seemed completely at peace and free from suffering. Siddhartha commanded his driver to stop so he could speak with the monk. "Who are you?" he asked, "How can you be content with the knowledge of this world around you?" The monk explained to the prince that he was a seeker of Truth, a seeker of life over death. To seek the Truth he had given up everything on this earth. Siddhartha decided that he, too, would seek the Truth in order to find peace. He would leave his riches, his family, and his protected life to follow in the monk's footsteps.

The night he was to leave the palace forever, his wife gave birth to a baby boy. Siddhartha was torn but knew he must follow his destiny, which did not include raising a child. He kissed his saddened family goodbye and ventured out from the kingdom. Once he was far off into the countryside, a monk appeared before the prince and offered him a robe and a begging bowl. The monk then disappeared. Siddhartha cut off his hair and cast away his princely garments. Now, alone with his few humble possessions, he began his quest for the Truth.

Along his journey he met with many monks and sought their wisdom, but none could teach him how to find the Truth of life over death and reach the state of absolute peace. Siddhartha met five hermits who denied their bodies any comfort in order to rise above earthly concerns. He remained six years with these men, eating very little and practicing rituals that caused him great pain. Close to starvation and death, he realized that he was still no closer to understanding the Truth. He decided that the Truth cannot be found in the mind or in the body but only in the innermost core of the heart which is connected to all existence. It was then that he decided to follow a middle path.

The hermits left Siddhartha in disgust for his weakness, and Siddartha traveled on in his quest. He accepted food from villagers and bathed in the river. Finally, he came to a large Bodhi tree. A cowherd offered him eight handfuls of grass to sit upon. Siddhartha spread the grass beneath the tree and vowed, "Even if my blood dries up and my skin and bones waste away, I will not leave this seat until I have found the Truth of life over death, the end of suffering for myself and for all people." Mara, the evil one, heard this vow and called on his army of demons to defeat Siddhartha's enlightenment. He plagued the prince with doubts and fears and called forth winds, rain, and lightening. No matter what evils the anti-god threw at him, Siddhartha remained pure in mind and meditated for 49 days.

At dawn on the fiftieth day, Siddhartha opened his eyes and glimpsed the last fading star. It was perfectly peaceful and the horizon glowed. At that moment Siddhartha became enlightened. Finally he could see the entire cycle of life and understand all of its mysteries. He saw the whole of existence within himself and himself the whole of existence. Rivers, once dry, began to flow, while flowers blossomed in the morning light. The animals danced and the birds all sang. Spirits, angels, and heavenly protectors were revealed with the scent of incense. At the age of 35, Siddhartha had ended his search. He had become Buddha, the enlightened one.

He left the shelter of the tree and set out to teach the Truth. He found the five hermits in a park near Sarnath and taught them the Four Noble Truths, the Eight-fold Path to follow, and the concept of *karma*, the cycle of death and rebirth measured by one's thoughts and deeds. The five hermits were doubtful at first of living the Middle Way but then became overwhelmed by the Buddha's wisdom and peace. They became his first disciples and spread his word. The Buddha traveled and taught his Truth of life over death.

The Legend of Buddha *(cont.)*

He taught meditations that helped purify body, speech, and mind. Eventually he had hundreds of followers from every walk of life, for he preached that anyone could reach enlightenment if he or she could find the path in his or her heart.

Buddha returned to his father's kingdom where he performed miracles to prove to the king that this was his chosen path. Many people in the kingdom, including his wife and son, were so moved that they left the comforts of the kingdom to follow him.

At the age of 80, after preaching for 45 years, the Buddha knew it was his time to die. Believing in reincarnation, he knew that the cycle of birth, suffering, death, and rebirth continues until enlightenment is gained. Most people travel through many lifetimes seeking this enlightenment. Siddhartha Gautama, the Buddha, had finally accomplished this feat and was finally free from further rebirth and earthly suffering. He had reached *nirvana*.

This story of Buddha's birth and life is legend, yet a man named Siddhartha Guatama did actually live in India from about 563 to 483 B.C. He traveled the countryside teaching others. His personal experiences and teachings are the foundation of Buddhism. At that time there was much unrest in India regarding religion, and many people who had begun to doubt the Vedic rituals that depended on priests, rules of caste, and animal sacrifices, were seeking spiritual answers.

Buddhism offered peace to everyone without the aid of priests and their rituals. It taught that all people were equal and that everyone had the right to a better life. Buddhism did not require animal sacrifices to gods, and it taught strict nonviolence against man and beast. The Buddha's teachings emphasized moderation in thought and action. Greed is wrong but so is complete denial of necessary comforts. Because it offered much to those seeking answers, Buddhism gained popularity, eventually becoming one of the world's leading religions.

Questions and Activities

1. What aspects of Buddhism seem similar to Hinduism? What aspects are different?

2. During the age of Siddhartha Gautama, there was much religious unrest. How did this affect the acceptance of Buddhism by the Indian people? Would there have been a different outcome had all people been satisfied with their religion?

3. Why did some people convert to the Buddhist religion? What kinds of people do you think converted? What did the religion offer them that the Aryan religion did not?

4. Who do you think would not convert to Buddhism from the Aryan society? Who would lose power with the introduction of this new religion?

5. How is the Buddha like other leaders of other religions? Research leaders such as Jesus, Mohammed, and Confucius. How are their lives similar? How are they different?

6. Photocopy pictures of Buddha from art books, encyclopedias, and other resources. Discuss the different ways artists of various cultures portray the Buddha. How are they similar? How are they different?

Basic Beliefs of Buddhism

Following his enlightenment, Buddha set forth the principles of his new religion, centered on how people should think and act. The basis of Buddhism lies in the Four Noble Truths, which explain why people suffer and how suffering can be avoided. By following the steps of the Eightfold Path, a Buddhist strives to become complete and reach enlightenment. Buddha called his path the Middle Way because it lies between luxury and unnecessary poverty.

As in Hinduism, *reincarnation*, the idea that the soul lives on after the body dies and is reborn in the body of another human or living form, and *karma* are central Buddhist beliefs. During each lifetime, the soul suffers and strives to reach enlightenment. The good or bad deeds performed within a lifetime, called *karma*, travel with the soul into the next life and determines one's fate. Good karma puts one closer to enlightenment while bad karma inflicts more suffering. This cycle is finally broken when one reaches enlightenment, like the Buddha. The soul then enters the state of *nirvana*, or highest bliss, and never returns to Earth again.

The tradition of Buddhism is made up of three components called the *Three Jewels*. The first jewel is the Buddha himself. The second jewel is *dharma*, the teachings of the Buddha, and the third is *sangha*, the community of believers, including monks, nuns, and other followers. Over time, devoted monks have built centers of religious study called monasteries where they practice the Buddha's way of life. Missionaries spread Buddhism across the world. Although it has become less popular in India over the years, Buddhism still remains a dominant world religion with over 250 million followers.

Activities:

1. Discuss the Four Noble Truths together as a class. Try to come up with examples for each of the truths that pertain to your life.

2. Research the Eightfold Path to discover the types of actions each path requires. How do we each follow these paths in our daily lives? What paths could we try harder to follow?

3. Once you have researched the Eightfold Path, compare it to other sets of laws in history. How is this similar to the Ten Commandments or Hammurabi's Code?

4. The wheel has become a major symbol in India. Legend claims that Buddha was born with the imprint of a wheel on both of his palms and on the soles of his feet. Buddhism uses the wheel to symbolize the setting in motion of Buddha's teachings, which are to roll onward. Write information describing the actions required by the Eightfold Path on the wheel diagram on the following page. Add color to the diagram and mount it on construction paper or poster board and display it on a bulletin board for others to view.

Basic Beliefs of Buddhism (cont.)

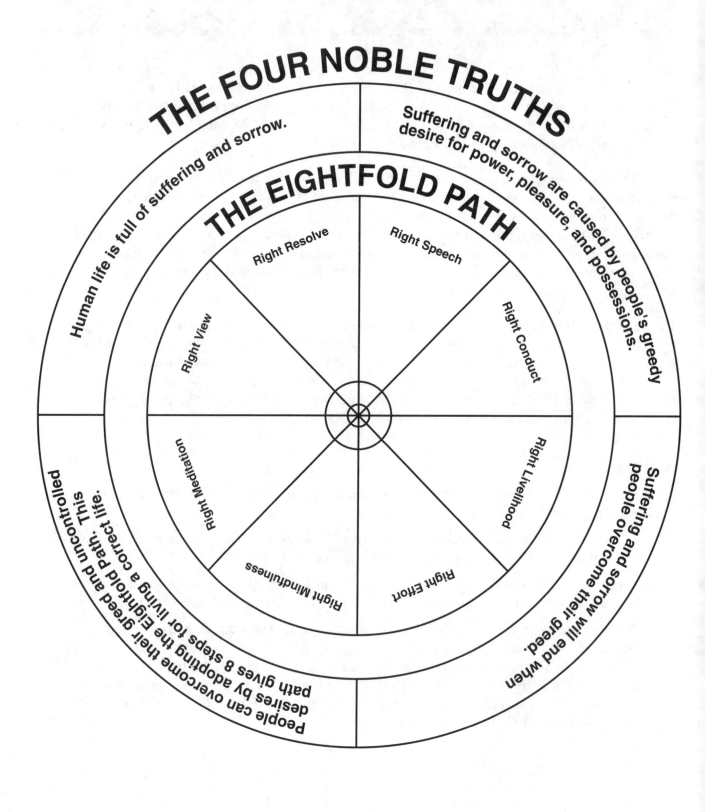

THE FOUR NOBLE TRUTHS

Human life is full of suffering and sorrow.

Suffering and sorrow are caused by people's greedy desire for power, pleasure, and possessions.

Suffering and sorrow will end when people overcome their greed.

People can overcome their greed and uncontrolled desires by adopting the Eightfold Path. This path gives 8 steps for living a correct life.

THE EIGHTFOLD PATH

Right Resolve

Right Speech

Right View

Right Conduct

Right Meditation

Right Livelihood

Right Mindfulness

Right Effort

Asoka's Edicts

The Mauryan Empire came to the height of its power in India under the rule of Asoka. Asoka had a powerful personality and military might. During his reign, the majority of the Indian subcontinent was conquered and ruled by the Mauryan Empire. However, following a brutal campaign against Kalinga, Asoka was filled with remorse and converted to the Buddhist religion which preached nonviolence.

From that time on he erected stone monuments containing his edicts, or laws, and inscriptions throughout the empire. Some were placed along the borders to show the vastness of his empire while others were placed along pilgrimage routes for Buddhists or at sites connected with the Buddha. There are monuments that describe Asoka's conversion to Buddhism and others that explain to the people his laws, which emphasized Buddhist ideals of tolerance, respect, social responsibility, and nonviolence.

One of Asoka's finest monuments was a pillar that stood at the deer park at Sarnath. This was the site where Buddha preached his first sermon called "The Turning of the Wheel of Law." The pillar was topped with a sculpture of four lions. Each lion looked in one of the four directions so that together their roar, like Buddha's teachings, could reach the four corners of the Earth. Originally the lions supported a huge wheel, the symbol of Buddha.

Asoka also traveled throughout his empire talking with the people and listening to their opinions. This was highly unusual behavior at this time for a ruler. He built roads, rest houses, hospitals, bathing tanks, and shady drinking places to make life easier for his people. He appointed special inspectors to travel throughout the land and make sure his reforms were in place.

Activities:

1. Asoka created lasting monuments to inform and teach his people of his laws and beliefs. What other historical figures carved their laws into stone for others to see? Research such people as Queen Hapshepsut of Egypt and Hammurabi of Babylon.

2. Research some of the monuments created by our government. What do these monuments have in common with Asoka's edicts in stone? What does this tell you about the need to put one's philosophies and beliefs into a lasting form? What do you think the monuments of our nation will be in 500 years?

3. Create your own edict. Use a sheet of construction paper to represent the sandstone monument. Cut it into your desired shape. Write your "laws," or philosophy on how to live your life right. Draw a picture at the top of the edict to represent your beliefs. Share your edict with the rest of the class and explain why you chose that particular symbol at the top.

Kalidasa and the Golden Age of India

The time of the Gupta Empire (A.D. 320–550) is often referred to as the golden age of India. This was a period when there was great growth in art, literature, education, religion, architecture, and science. Empire boundaries expanded and trade routes hummed with activity throughout the Mediterranean, Africa, China, Asia, and Indonesia. Usually such growth takes place when there is a strong government, or a large group of wealthy, educated citizens, or during a time of peace. During the long reign of the Gupta rulers, India enjoyed all three of these conditions.

During this period Indians took up an active religious life. Hinduism returned as the dominant religion since the Gupta rulers were Hindus. Buddhism was also tolerated and practiced by many citizens. Many spectacular and ornate monuments and temples were built during this age to honor both religions. Some of these temples came to be considered especially holy and were supported by people both rich and poor. Their money helped to pay for sculptures, priests, musicians, and dancers who performed the religious ceremonies. Some of the larger temples also set up schools and hospitals.

Since Gupta India became a center of learning, visitors from other parts of Asia came to learn and share ideas. In Hindu schools and Buddhist monasteries, students learned grammar, mathematics, medicine, philosophy, and religious writings. The greatest contributions of Gupta scholars were in the fields of science and math. Indian doctors were the first to develop innoculation against disease. Surgeons sterilized tools, knew how to set bones, and repaired facial features with plastic surgery. Indian astronomers determined that the world was round and rotated around the sun, facts unaccepted by Europeans until 1,000 years later. Astronomers also calculated the solar year at 365.358 days, a figure off by only three hours. It was the Gupta mathematicians who invented the base ten decimal system and the numerals 1 to 9 that we use today, called Arabic numbers. They also developed the concepts of zero and infinity.

The arts also flourished under Gupta rule. Musicians and dancers developed forms that are now the basis for classical Indian music and dance. Sculptors and painters worked diligently on art for the temples and monuments. Some of the finest examples of art from this period were found inside the Buddhist cave temples of Ajanta in West India.

Great works of literature were written during the period in Sanskrit, the language reserved for only the highest castes. The *Bhagavad-Gita* was an important book in Gupta times. Its title means "Song of the Blessed One." It was part of a larger body of work written hundreds of years earlier called the *Mahabharata* which had been rewritten by the Guptas to include Hindu concepts. The *Gita* tells of a warrior's duty to fulfill his destiny even though he questions killing others. This story helps reinforce the Hindu concept of *dharma*, or fulfilling one's caste duties without question or complaint. As the god Krishna explains in the *Bhagavad-Gita*, "There is more joy in doing one's own duty badly than in doing another man's duty well."

Kalidasa and the Golden Age of India *(cont.)*

One of the greatest writers of this time was Kalidasa. He was a playwright and poet for the court of Chandra Gupta II (A.D. 380–415). The following are some lines from his famous play *Shakuntala* in which a queen tries to bring back her noble husband's memory.

Shakuntala: *Do you not remember in the jasmine-bower, one day, how you had poured the rainwater that a lotus had collected in its cups into the hollow of your hand?*

King: *I am listening, tell on.*

Shakuntala: *Just then, my adopted child, the little fawn, ran up with long, soft eyes . . . and you, before you quenched your own thirst, gave to the little creature, saying, 'Drink you first, gentle fawn.'*

The poems and plays of Kalidasa expressed a wide range of emotions, called *rasas*, and helped reinforce Hindu concepts. The *rasas* included eight emotions: happiness, sadness, anger, pride, love, fear, loathing, and wonder. Choose one of the *rasas* to write a poem of your own following the given directions.

Write a Poem Like Kalidasa

1. Fold a sheet of writing paper into eight boxes. In each box write one of the eight emotions, or *rasas*. Next, in each box, record images that the emotion evokes. What makes you happy? What makes you proud? What makes you angry? etc.

2. Choose one of the emotions to write about in your poem. On the back of the paper, record the chosen emotion. Brainstorm how this emotion affects each of your senses. What do you see? What do you smell? What do you touch, feel, taste, and hear?

3. Elaborate on each of the senses to build phrases and sentences. Try to use a variety of figurative language techniques such as metaphors, similes, personification, and alliteration. Use a thesaurus to help build your poetic vocabulary.

4. Combine the phrases to create your poem. Remember, a poem does not need to rhyme. An example has been provided for you.

Happiness at the Sea

As I dive carelessly into the cool, blue sea,
The smooth sultry seaweed caresses each gleaming limb, playfully tugging and pulling.
The soft, rippling water echoes of dancing porpoises,
Singing their songs of joy like gay mermaids.
Gulls soar overhead, squawking to join the chorus as they dip and dive into the waves.
I emerge from the sapphire abyss.
Salty water tingles along my face like the flow of a smooth silk scarf.
Below, the sandy floor squishes and tickles between my toes,
As I leap to shore one soggy step after another.
I glance back at the vast blue sea as it shimmers in the afternoon sun,
Reflecting smiling dimples of gray, green, and violet.
Contentment fills me along the shore of this beautiful ocean.

Islam in India

The Islamic religion was founded by an Arab named Mohammed, who was born in A.D. 570 in the town of Mecca. *Islam* is an Arabic term that means both "submission to God" and "peace." Followers of this religion are called *Muslims*, or "those who have submitted to God." Islam is the second-largest religious group in modern India, comprising about 11 percent of the population.

When Mohammed was growing up in Arabia, people worshipped many gods and idols. Mohammed had a vision in which God spoke to him through the angel Gabriel. He was told that it was up to him to preach a new religion to the others in his country. This new religion would honor only one god whom he called *Allah*. Other divine messages came to Mohammed from God and were eventually recorded in the sacred text known as the *Koran*.

Every Muslim must follow certain basic principles enshrined in the Koran. He must profess his faith in Allah, the one ultimate God. He must recite prayers five times a day facing the holy town of Mecca. He must fast during the month of Ramadan, a holy holiday. He must give part of his wealth to charity and make a pilgrimage to Mecca at least once in his lifetime, if he can afford it.

Mohammed ventured out and taught this new religion to his people. The Islamic religion taught equality, brotherhood, compassion, and mercy. Before he died in A.D. 632, Mohammed had become a great political and military leader as well as a religious one. His followers then set out to carry his message to neighboring lands by force. By A.D. 670, Arabian Muslims had conquered Iraq, Iran, Turkey, and all of northern Africa. Over the next few centuries, Muslims made raids into India. By 1206, Delhi was ruled by Muslim *sultans*, or kings. From there the Muslim leaders worked their way east and south, converting lower caste Hindus to Islam.

Mughal is the Indian word for *Mongol*, a person from the north Asian country of Mongolia. The word has changed meaning over the years to refer to the Islamic Moguls who ruled India from 1526 to 1707. The Moguls displaced the weaker sultans to create a long and prosperous Mogul Empire. Under the Moguls, Hindu and Muslim traditions combined to make important contributions in poetry, music, and architecture.

The Muslim rule in India collapsed after 550 years and was replaced by the British. By the twentieth century, tensions between Muslims and Hindus led to the division of India into two countries: Pakistan, which is now a purely Islamic state, and India, which is the secular state where freedom of religion is practiced.

Questions and Activities:

1. How is the founding of Islam similar to the founding of Christianity? How are Jesus and Mohammed alike? Bethlehem and Mecca? Research further to find other interesting similarities between these two religions. Research the Christian Crusades to learn about a clash between the religions. What do we learn by studying history and religion? How can we avoid making the same mistakes?

2. During the spread of Islam throughout India, it was usually the lower caste Indians who converted. Why do you think this was the case? What did Islam offer them that Hinduism did not? How is this similar to those who converted to Buddhism?

Compare the Great Mogul Emperors

During the sixteenth century, much of India came under the control of Muslims from the northwest. These were the mighty Moguls who succeeded in establishing one of the most splendid and powerful empires ever seen. The Mogul Empire became famous for the grandeur of its courts and palaces, gardens, building projects, art, and literature. It also became known for the six strongest rulers, known as the Great Moguls. These rulers began to explore India in detail and established brilliant systems of communication and administration. Use resource materials to complete the chart below comparing the Great Mogul Leaders.

Name	Dates Ruled	Leadership Style	Contributions to Indian Culture
Babur			
Humayun			
Akbar			
Jahangir			
Shah Jahan			
Aurangzeb			

Writing Activity:

If you could be a Mogul Emperor, which leader would you choose to be? Write a persuasive composition describing the leader of your choice. Give at least three supporting arguments from your research for your choice. Make sure your composition is organized with an opening statement, your supporting arguments, and a strong closing statement. Share compositions as a class to see which leader was most popular.

Europeans in India

In addition to Muslims, other foreigners visited India in the thirteenth and fourteenth centuries. Accounts of their travels are valuable records of the early Muslim rule in India. Their tales also inspired later explorers, especially Europeans, who began arriving in India during the fifteenth and sixteenth centuries. These explorers had heard unbelievable stories describing the wealth of the East, and they came in search of trade. The Europeans sought to deal directly with India, cutting out the Arabian middlemen who controlled trading and profits. Portuguese, Dutch, and English traders established companies to trade for various goods, including spices, fabrics, and dyes. Match the following Europeans with their exploits in India.

Marco Polo (*Italy*) Ralph Fitch (*Britain*) Niccolo dei Conti (*Italy*)

Niccolo Manucci (*Italy*) Athanasius Nikitin (*Russia*) Thomas Roe (*Britain*)

Vasco de Gama (*Portugal*)

1. _____ He set off to India from Russia in 1468 and was the only European to visit the chief city of Muslim India at that time. He was despondent at the contrast between the rich and the poor of India. His travel accounts were recorded in 1475.

2. _____ England's first ambassador to India, he spent four years at Jahangir's court, from 1615–1619, after he was sent by King James I to seek a trade treaty. His memoirs described a strange birthday custom of the Emperor Jahangir, who would weigh himself against sacks of gold and jewels to be distributed among the people.

3. _____ A Portuguese navigator, he was the first European to reach India by sea in 1497. He brought home precious spices which spurred a great influx of traders from Portugal.

4. _____ He traveled with his father through Turkey, Persia, and Afghanistan, crossing into India through the Hindu Kush Mountains to join the Old Silk Road to China in 1271. Considered one of the most adventurous explorers in the East, his exploits inspired many other explorers, such as Christopher Columbus.

5. _____ This Italian who visited southern India in the early fifteenth century was amazed by the king's vast harem that followed him wherever he went. During his 25 years in India, he witnessed many wars and the rite of *sati* in which wives throw themselves on their husbands' burning funeral pyres.

6. _____ He arrived in India at the age of 17 from his home in Venice, Italy, and remained there for 61 years until his death. As a youth he joined the fighting between rival Mogul brothers and eventually fought on both sides. After military life, he practiced medicine although he had no formal training. He became the royal physician, was knighted by the Portuguese government, and then served the English governor as a correspondent between the English and a Mogul leader.

7. _____ He was one of the first English merchants to arrive in India in 1583. He delivered letters to the Mogul Emperor from Queen Elizabeth I. During his travels he was imprisoned for spying and witnessed the world famous diamonds of Golconda.

Answers (*cover before coying*)

1. Athanasius Nikitin 2. Thomas Roe 3. Vasco de Gama 4. Marco Polo 5. Niccolo dei Conti 6. Niccolo Manucci
7. Ralph Fitch

Jains and Sikhs

Vardhamana Jnatiputra was the son of a rich and powerful chief who lived in northern India in the sixth century B.C. Like Siddartha Gautama, he grew up in luxury but questioned the meaning of life and his destiny. When he was 30 his parents died, and he became a holy man wandering about the country practicing self-denial as a means of discipline and purification of the spirit. He debated the issues of life and death with other holy men he met. He became a persuasive preacher. His followers called him *Mahavira*, the Great Hero, and considered him the last of the 24 founders or prophets of the path. He was also called *Jina*, one who has conquered the senses, and the name *Jainism* came from this title.

Mahavira reinterpreted the fundamental principles of Hinduism, such as karma and reincarnation. He urged his followers to cleanse the soul by getting rid of all earthly desires and evil behavior, and he taught strict physical and mental discipline and a rigorous code of morality, self denial, and nonviolence. Jains consider killing any living creature the greatest sin. They carry a small broom to clear the path where they walk and wear face masks to avoid killing germs through breathing. Jains cannot be farmers, since tilling the soil might kill creatures living in the earth.

Like Buddhists, the followers of Jainism do not believe in a personal God. They believe that perfect wisdom is obtained through the right faith, the right knowledge, and the right conduct. Although only 4 million citizens in southern India practice the Jain religion, it has contributed to the social and cultural life of the country. Many Hindu practices, such as vegetarianism and fasting, are Jain in origin.

✧ ✧ ✧ ✧ ✧

Guru (teacher) Nanak lived in the Punjab region of northwestern India from 1469–1539. Nanak, a Hindu, had many close Muslim friends and studied the similarities between the two religions. He visited Hindu holy places and made a pilgrimage to Mecca with his Muslim friends. He began to preach a new message which rejected caste and religious distinctions. He taught the doctrine of one God, which he simply called *Ikk*, or "One." He believed that God could be perceived through loving devotion and a brotherhood uniting Muslims with all castes of Hindus. His followers called themselves *Sikhs*, a Sanskrit word meaning disciple.

Sikhism grew under the fourth teacher, Ram Das, who constructed the Golden Temple at Amritsar, the holiest shrine of the Sikhs. The holy scripture of the Sikhs, compiled by Guru Arjun, is called *Granth Sahib*, or *The Book of the Lord*. Later, Sikhs were persecuted by Muslims and Hindus. Guru Gobind gave Sikhism the martial direction it needed for self-defense. In 1699, he founded the *Khalasa* (pure), a religious and military fraternity which Sikh men are expected to join. They observe the five K's which include not cutting their hair or beards, and wearing a comb in their hair, a steel bracelet on their right wrists, soldier's shorts, and carrying a steel dagger. All Sikh men use the last name Singh, which means "lion," to show that they are good warriors.

Sikhs believe strongly in one god. They reject the Hindu caste system but accept the concepts of karma and rebirth. Sikh rituals and practices are much like Hindu rituals, and intermarriage between the two religions is common. However, since 1980 tension has been growing, and an extreme Sikh group has been calling for an independent Sikh homeland called Khalistan, meaning "Land of the Pure."

Activity: Compare and discuss India's main religions. Use the directions and chart on page 59 to aid with the comparison.

A Letter Home to England

Much like the Hindu caste system, British society in India was divided into a rigid order. The highest class consisted of the high government officials, followed by army officers, the business people, the ordinary soldiers, and finally the Indian people. Some of the British socialized with the Indians in the upper class, like princes, but for the most part they kept to themselves and maintained a lifestyle like they would have had in England.

Read Chapter 5 of *Exploration Into India*. Pretend that you are one of the upper class British women relocated to India, and write a letter home to your mother describing your new life in India. Tell about your daily routine, your family, your servants, your husband's occupation and leisure activities, upcoming events, and the interesting sights and people you have seen. Are you happy in India? Discuss your aspirations for yourself and your family as you close your letter.

April 14, 1879

Dear Mother, _____

_____

_____

_____

_____

_____

_____

_____

_____

_____

_____

_____

_____

_____

_____

_____

_____

Gaining Independence

Toward the end of the nineteenth century, a new nationalist reform movement began to take hold in India. This movement eventually led to the independence of India in 1947, but with a high cost to Hindus, British, and Muslims. Research the following key figures, organizations, and events to learn their roles in India's struggle for independence. Complete the activity at the bottom of the page.

1. Mohandas Gandhi _____

   _____

2. Lord Mountbatten _____

   _____

3. Jawaharlal Nehru _____

   _____

4. Aga Khan _____

   _____

5. Mohammed Ali Jinnah _____

   _____

6. Indian National Congress _____

   _____

7. Muslim League _____

   _____

8. Rowlatt Acts of 1918 _____

   _____

9. Massacre of 1919 at a Hindu festival _____

   _____

10. The Partition of India _____

   _____

Activity:

After researching the road to independence, work with two other friends to write personal diary accounts describing the feelings of the people in India during this tumultuous time. Each member of the group will write from a different viewpoint: a British officer, a Hindu, or a Muslim. Describe the different people and events from this time period from your perspective. Share your diary entries and compare the feelings of the different people. How did each group succeed in getting what they wanted? What did each group lose?

Extension:

Choose one of the major figures from the list above and learn more about his life before, during, and after India's independence. Report your findings to the class.

Tusk and Stone

by Malcolm Bosse

Summary

Tusk and Stone describes the excitement and torment of living in 7th century India through the eyes of a boy reaching manhood. Arjun, a scholar from the highest Brahman class, is traveling with a caravan when it is ambushed by *dacoits*, or bandits.   Although he escapes alive, all the others are slaughtered or kidnapped, including his mute younger sister. Arjun is drugged and sold to the army as a slave where he gains status as a *mahout* riding on the back of an elephant in battle. His bravery brings fame, and his quest for his sister is spread through songs. Injured by a vengeful army sergeant, Arjun is left for dead after a battle. Nursed back to health by the enemy, Arjun again tries to make the best of his life, becoming a carver and sculptor of stone. As Arjun's travels take the reader across central and southern India, the reader is exposed to the religious and cultural environment of medieval India.

This outline is a suggested plan for using the various activities that are presented in this book. Each of the lessons can take from one to several days to complete.

Sample Plan

Lesson 1
- ❏ Complete one or more of the Setting the Stage activities on page 25.
- ❏ Make journals, following the directions on page 78.
- ❏ Review the map, physical and cultural references, and vocabulary activities contained in the journals.
- ❏ Read and discuss Hindu beliefs, page 55.
- ❏ Complete the Hindu Gods Identity Cards, pages 56–58.

Lesson 2
- ❏ Read chapter 1 of *Tusk and Stone*.
- ❏ Begin defining Indian vocabulary, page 41.
- ❏ Record physical and cultural references, page 27.
- ❏ Begin mapping Arjun's travels, page 51.
- ❏ Map trade routes, page 60.
- ❏ Compare and contrast life stages, page 43.

Lesson 3
- ❏ Read chapters 2–4.
- ❏ Continue journal activities.
- ❏ Complete the Figurative Language activity, page 28.
- ❏ Read about the Indian Caste System, pages 7–8.
- ❏ Complete the caste system activity, page 9.
- ❏ Write a letter about army life, page 29.
- ❏ Discuss Arjun's Destiny and write about your own destiny, page 30.

Lesson 4
- ❏ Read chapters 5–9.
- ❏ Continue journal activities.
- ❏ Answer the Know Your Elephant questions, page 31.
- ❏ Describe, draw, and name your own war elephant, page 32.

Lesson 5
- ❏ Read chapters 10–11.
- ❏ Continue journal activities.
- ❏ Read and discuss the Legend of Buddha, pages 10–12.

- ❏ Complete activities on Buddhism, page 13.
- ❏ Create a cave painting, page 68.
- ❏ Write a persuasive paragraph, page 33.
- ❏ Compare India's major religions, page 59.

Lesson 6
- ❏ Read chapters 12–14.
- ❏ Continue journal activities.
- ❏ Write about your first battle experience, page 34.
- ❏ Make A Classroom *Rig-Veda*, page 42.
- ❏ Read about Kalidasa and write poems, pages 16–17.

Lesson 7
- ❏ Read chapters 15–18.
- ❏ Continue journal activities.
- ❏ Draw and decorate a royal elephant, page 67.
- ❏ Make a procession bulletin board, page 35.
- ❏ Describe a Maharajah's life, page 46–47.
- ❏ Note and illustrate the changes in Arjun, page 37.
- ❏ Check your comprehension, page 38.

Lesson 8
- ❏ Read chapters 19–21.
- ❏ Continue journal activities.
- ❏ Design an Ancient Indian City, page 61.
- ❏ Complete the Friend or Foe activity, page 39.
- ❏ Make a relief sculpture, page 68.
- ❏ Explore Indian Myths and Tales, pages 44–45.

Lesson 9
- ❏ Read Chapters 22–25.
- ❏ Continue journal activities.
- ❏ Experiment with meditation, page 64.
- ❏ Write a New Ending, page 40.
- ❏ Prepare a time line of India, pages 62–63.
- ❏ Complete one or more culminating activities, pages 70–77.

Overview of Activities

Setting the Stage

1. Assemble the Ancient India Bulletin Board (page 78) for students to complete as the unit progresses.

2. Make literature journals (page 78) to keep all notes and handouts organized for reference throughout the unit. Review the different pages included in the folder to be used after each reading assignment—the map to trace the route of Arjun, the vocabulary lists, and the physical and cultural environment chart.

3. Have students brainstorm what they already know about India—famous people, food, animals, religions, customs, geography, dress, language, etc. Write these ideas on the board. Introduce students to the land and people of India by reviewing the social studies text, encyclopedias, and other resource materials on India.

4. Show students the cover of the book. Ask them to predict from the title and the cover art what the story is about.

5. Tell students that the story *Tusk and Stone* takes place in 7th century India after the end of the Great Gupta Empire. At that time India consisted of small kingdoms with no main kingdom unifying the nation. These small kingdoms fought one another for land and holdings. It was a time of turmoil, excitement, and change.

6. Introduce students to Arjun, the main character of the story. Ask students how they would feel if they were ambushed on their first day of high school, taken from everyone and everything that they knew, and forced to join the army. This is what happened to Arjun, and they will follow his adventures as he travels and discovers life in India, as well as discovering himself.

Enjoying the Book

1. Begin by reading the first chapter only of *Tusk and Stone*. Discuss the economy and trade of India and the use of caravans. Have students make a Trade Route Map (page 60) to better understand the aspects of travel in 7th Century India and the merging of many different people.

2. Throughout the story, Hinduism is the main religion although Buddhism is also referenced. To help students understand references to Hindu gods and religious practices, have them read and discuss Hindu beliefs (page 55) and complete the Hindu Gods Identity Cards (pages 56–58). Use the cards to play a form of Concentration, matching details to names and pictures. You may wish to have the students assemble the cards as a reference booklet or combine them with other pages and activities in this book to create a book of Indian religions.

3. Play some Indian music. Look for tapes or CDs by sitarist Ravi Shankar, especially *Sounds of India*. You may wish to explain to the students that Shankar influenced the Beatles and that many people explored Indian culture and philosophy as part of the "hippie" era. Discuss the role of music in Arjun's life and quest.

4. Have students compare the life stages of Arjun and his people to their own. In what stage is Arjun? What do they think his future holds?

Overview of Activities *(cont.)*

Enjoying the Book *(cont.)*

5. After each reading assignment, have students use their literature journal to map the route Arjun is taking through India. Assign appropriate words from the vocabulary list that correspond to each reading assignment and have students record on their charts details about the environment and culture of India that were found in the literature. Discuss these findings together as a class.

6. Complete other lessons and activities listed in the Sample Plan which correspond to each reading selection.

Extending the Book

1. After completing the book, have students create new endings for the story that deal with different outcomes and different versions of Arjun's destiny and duty (page 40).

2. Review the facts about India's physical and cultural environment that were gathered while reading the book. What did the book discuss in length? (military/government, elephants, philosophy, religion, the caste system, geography, etc.) What aspects of Indian culture were neglected? (family life, occupations and lifestyles of the different people in different levels of the caste system, role of women and children, etc.)

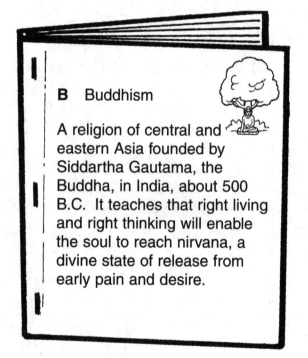

B Buddhism

A religion of central and eastern Asia founded by Siddartha Gautama, the Buddha, in India, about 500 B.C. It teaches that right living and right thinking will enable the soul to reach nirvana, a divine state of release from early pain and desire.

3. This book described one period in the history of India. India has been shaped by many different people migrating from many different regions. Have students complete the Time Line of India (page 62) and/or the ABC Picture Book of India (page 70) to get a better overview of the changes that have taken place in India.

4. Prepare a list of individuals, events, and topics from Indian history. Group the students and ask each group to select a topic to research. Ask them to prepare a presentation on their topic to share with the class. They may choose to dramatize it, create a newspaper, etc.

5. Plan a Day in Ancient India to celebrate the wonders of India (page 72). Students could perform their Caste System Dramas (page 71) as one of the activities for the day.

6. Read more about India and the many different people who call it home. Ask students to describe what they find most fascinating about India and what they feel is the most difficult to understand. What have the people of India brought to our country? How can we enjoy our knowledge of India in our daily lives?

Physical and Cultural Environment Charts

Although the story of Arjun and his travels across 7th Century India is fiction, many historical facts and descriptions of physical and cultural aspects of life in India are included in the book. Have students make charts like the ones below on sheets of white writing paper to include in their journals.

As you read each section of the book, have students note the details about India mentioned in the text. Record the page numbers where the information was found and discuss the findings as a class. If desired, have selected students research and share information about topics mentioned in the book that have not already been taught in class.

At the end of the unit, discuss how much you learned about India without reading a social studies text. Discuss what aspects of India were not included in the book, as well.

native plants and trees	wild animals
domesticated animals	food and spices
medicine and narcotics	geography and climate

religious customs	education
poetry and literature	music and art
modes of transportation	economy: imports and exports

military	leaders and government
social classes	occupations or Jati
customs based on caste	clothing

Figurative Language

Malcolm Bosse uses a variety of figurative language techniques to paint a vivid picture of life in medieval India. Read the following quotations from the story and then write the message the author is trying to convey.

Simile: Making a comparison between two objects or ideas using the words "like" or "as."

Metaphor: Making a comparison between two objects or ideas.

Personification: Giving person-like characteristics to ideas or objects.

1. *Simile:* "He'd like to get the day's march over with, instead of shuffling along like a sleepy cow."
   _____

2. *Metaphor:* "Just then a large swamp bird rose out of the sedge, its black wings beating with the heavy report that women make when they slap wet laundry against a rock."
   _____

3. *Simile:* "Gauri looked at him (the leader of the dacoits) as if he were nothing more than a tree."
   _____

4. *Personification and Simile:* "Fog was churning around legs and arms until they vanished from the clearing like bushes lost from view in a monsoon storm."
   _____

5. *Simile:* "Dacoits these days are as thick as centipedes in a log." _____
   _____

Activity:

Describe the following scenes using the type of figurative language technique mentioned.

1. seeing the tiger (simile) _____
   _____

2. the day after the dacoit attack (metaphor)_____
   _____

3. waking to find yourself in the army (simile)_____
   _____

4. learning the weapons of war (personification) _____
   _____

You're in the Army Now!

Imagine that you have been drugged and taken into the army against your will, like Arjun. Write a letter home describing your new life to your family. Use the descriptions in the book and the vocabulary below to tell of your daily routines and training. Draw a picture of yourself with your military uniform, armor, and weapons on the page to accompany the letter.

Weapons	Infantry	Cavalry
mace battle axe two handed swords (*khadga*) *chakras* (ninja disks) bow and arrow metal tipped *bhallas* three-pointed lance (*trisula*) dagger pike tomara catapults battering rams (*tortoise*)	bowman lancer battle formations battle signals, cries, flags	horse and chariot elephants mahout ankus battle formations battle signals

May 23, A.D. 647

Dear Bapu (Dad), _____

_____

_____

_____

_____

_____

_____

_____

_____

_____

Arjun's Destiny

In the Hindu religion there are three main components that guide one's path through life, or destiny.

Reincarnation: Life is a ceaseless cycle of events with no beginning or end. Death and birth are just phases in the cycle. Each person must live several lives or be reincarnated over and over again on Earth, reaching higher and higher social levels before reaching the final supreme goal of Absolute, called *moksha*. Once this goal is achieved, the soul is released, never to come to Earth again.

Karma: Everything a person does has a consequence. Both good and bad deeds have an effect on a person's happiness or misery in his or her present life, as well as on future lives. One's destiny in this life is guided by the good and bad deeds performed in the present life, as well as those of previous lives. Good karma leads to reincarnation on a higher social level while bad karma results in a lower social level for the next life. Karma helps to explain the inequalities of life, such as why one man is born poor or handicapped or suffers a series of hardships, while another enjoys peace and prosperity.

Dharma: One is born into a particular station in life, and it is his or her moral duty to live according to that station. The person should go about daily life without question or complaint, fulfilling his or her duty to society at that particular social level. An individual who respects the caste system, social customs, and laws in this life will be rewarded in the next life with a higher social position. Because of this, Hindus passively accept poverty or misfortunes as their duty.

Throughout chapters 1–4 of *Tusk and Stone* there are many references to Arjun's destiny, duty, and karma. After recording all of the references you can find in the spaces below, answer the questions that follow on the back of this paper.

	Page Number
Destiny References	
Duty (Dharma) References	
Karma References	

1. What do you think Arjun's family believed his destiny to be?

2. Why did Arjun accept his kidnapping into the army and reject his Brahman class?

3. How does Arjun's sense of karma guide his daily choices and attitude?

4. What do you feel is your destiny? What do you believe will decide this destiny?

5. What actions do you feel are your duty to perform? How does a sense of duty to your family, school, and country shape your everyday actions?

Know Your Elephant

After reading chapters 5–9 of *Tusk and Stone*, imagine that you have been selected to be a mahout on one of the elephants of the cavalry. Before you can be selected, you must pass the elephant test by answering these questions on a separate sheet of paper. Work in small groups and use the book as your guide. The group with the most correct answers will become the new mahouts!

Chapter 5

1. Describe the elephant's sense of touch, smell, and sight.
2. How much does an elephant eat?
3. Why must you protect an elephant's skin?
4. Describe the speed and movements of an elephant.
5. Is an elephant loyal to its master?

Chapter 6

1. What does an elephant do when it meets another elephant?
2. Describe the different ways in which the elephant communicates with noise and gestures.
3. What does it mean when an elephant holds it head high?
4. Can elephants swim? If so, how?
5. What is the best way to control an elephant?

Chapter 7

1. What is built to catch wild elephants?
2. Why does one escape an angry elephant by leading him to a hill?
3. How are the elephants led into the corral?

Chapter 8

1. What are *koomkies*?
2. How are the wild elephants subdued in order to begin training them?
3. What can elephants smell on their handlers?
4. Why is persistent beating more important than painful beating when training your elephant?
5. What is the Great Shaking?

Chapter 9

1. How do you know when your elephant has finally surrendered to you?
2. Who was the elephant Airavata?
3. Describe the ceremony of becoming a mahout.

Naming Your Gaja

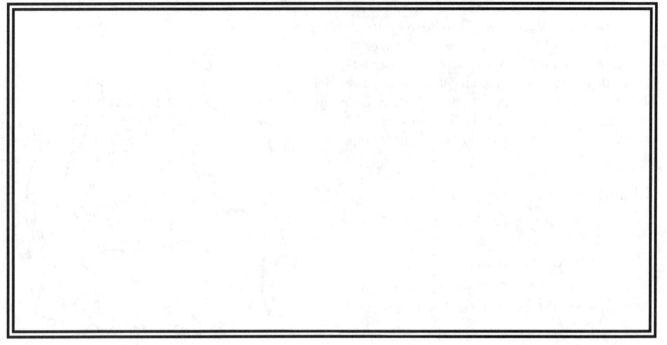

Congratulations! You have been selected to join the ranks of the mahouts. You have been given an elephant to train and name. Draw a picture of your new gaja and answer the questions below.

1. Describe your gaja's size, color, texture, and strength.

   _____

   _____

2. Describe your gaja's personality.

   _____

   _____

3. What is your philosophy on training your gaja? What techniques do you plan to use to make your gaja obey you?

   _____

   _____

   _____

4. What did you name your gaja? Why did you choose that name?

   _____

   _____

Boot Camp Persuasive Writing

In chapter 10 Arjun has a showdown with his commanding officer, Vasu. Vasu is humiliated and threatens to kill Arjun someday. Do you think it was right for Arjun to question the authority of Vasu?

Use the persuasive writing organizer below to write a composition describing your feelings. Share your composition with others in the class. What did the majority of the class feel was the correct action to take?

Introduction (Tell some background information about the situation. Describe the issue and your position for or against Arjun's actions.)

List three reasons for your position and provide supporting details for each one.

Reason	Supporting Details
1.	
2.	
3.	

Conclusion (Summarize your reasons and give a convincing closing statement.)

Extensions:

1. Hold a class debate concerning Arjun's actions.

2. Have students present their compositions as speeches. Tell them to pretend that they are Arjun's friend telling him why he must follow his instincts or why he should listen to Vasu.

Your First Look at War

In chapters 12–14 Arjun gets his first taste of real war. Nothing could have prepared him for the feelings and actions that took place during the few days of battle.

Imagine that you are a soldier with Arjun fighting your very first battle. Write journal entries to describe your feelings leading up to the battle, your feelings during the battle, and your feelings and attitude about war after the battle. Use the book and the questions below to help organize your thoughts.

Before the Battle:

1. What training exercises are physically preparing you for the battle? _____

   _____

2. What steps are you taking to prepare yourself emotionally or spiritually? _____

   _____

3. What do you imagine the fighting will be like? _____

   _____

4. How do you think you will handle the onset of fighting, both emotionally and physically?

   _____

During the Battle:

1. How did the fighting begin? What set it off? _____

   _____

2. What sounds can you hear during the battle? What do you smell? _____

   _____

3. Describe some of the fighting you see directly around you. _____

   _____

4. What are you actually doing during the battle? What do you feel? _____

   _____

5. How does the battle end? _____

After the Battle:

1. Describe the scene after the battle. What do you see now on the battle ground? What do you smell and hear? _____

   _____

2. How do you feel now about the battle? Was it worth the fight? Are you filled with a sense of victory or disappointment? _____

   _____

3. How will you cope with what you did and saw? _____

   _____

4. What meaning does war now have for you? _____

   _____

Military Procession Bulletin Board

Military life is described in detail throughout *Tusk and Stone*. One of the most fascinating descriptions is the detailed account of the procession heading across India for military conquest. Have your students depict this vast procession of people and animals on one of your classroom bulletin boards by drawing and cutting out figures using the patterns on the next page.

Activity:

1. Cover a bulletin board with black or dark blue paper. Label the board "A Military Procession Across India."

2. Tell students that they will be working together to create a picture of what an Indian military procession may have looked like as it made its way through the Indian countryside. Review some of the descriptions in chapter 12 (the cavalry and procession line-up) and chapter 15 (the harem in procession) in class. Discuss and list on the chalkboard the components of the procession.

3. Draw a diagram like the one below on a chalkboard or overhead projector. Assign groups of students to different portions of the procession.

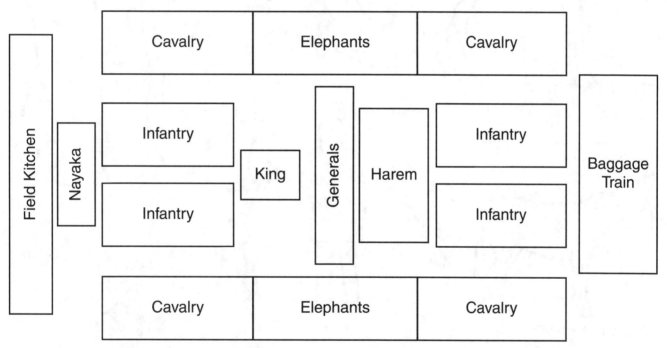

4. Reproduce and distribute the generic patterns on the following page. You may wish to enlarge them. Ask the students to add the details that are appropriate for their figures like weapons, uniforms (all military should be in red), props, etc. Have all figures colored brightly and then cut out.

5. Have students draw and cut out other objects such as weapons and carts to be pulled by the horses and oxen. Add any other features you choose to the procession.

6. Assemble the procession by stapling the figures to the bulletin board in the appropriate places. Add labels to the different sections of the procession. Have students describe what it must have been like to travel with such a large group of people and animals. What would meals be like? Sleeping? Using the restroom? Ask each student where in the procession he or she would most like to be.

Military Procession Bulletin Board

(cont.)

Reproduce as many generic figures as you need to use as patterns for your bulletin board.

horse

elephant corps

harem

donkeys

servants/footmen

cavalry officers

infantry

oxen

king/nayaka

36

©*Teacher Created Materials, Inc.*

Arjun, Before and After

Arjun went through many transformations throughout the story. After Arjun's brave exploits in chapter 17, he was asked what he wanted as his reward. To the king's astonishment, he desired a magnificent costume so that his enemies would single him out. Find the description of Arjun in the first chapter as he began his journey. Record the description and page number. Add details to the figure to make it match the description. Do the same for Arjun as he appears in chapter 17. With your class discuss all of the changes that happened to Arjun along the way.

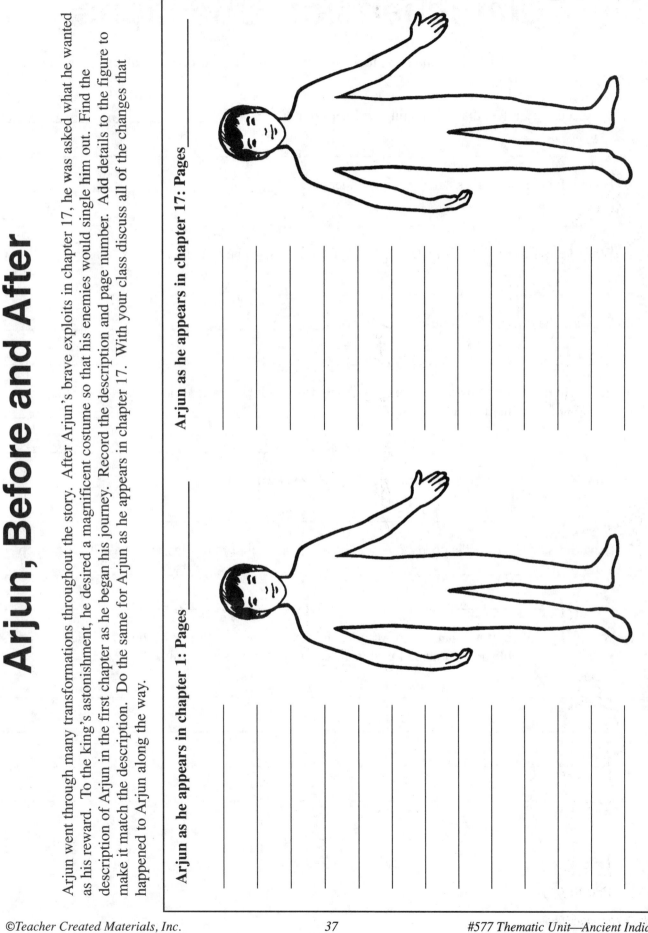

Arjun as he appears in chapter 1: Pages _____

Arjun as he appears in chapter 17: Pages _____

Comprehension Questions

After reading chapters 15–18, use the book to answer the following questions about Arjun, his actions, and his future.

1. Why does Arjun feel that his fighting will help find his sister? _____

   _____

2. How will his new clothes help with this endeavor? _____

   _____

3. What do you think Arjun is really searching for that cannot be found with his sister? _____

   _____

4. Why are the other soldiers upset with Arjun? _____

   _____

5. Earlier in the story Arjun is threatened by Vasu, foreshadowing a terrible defeat for Arjun. How does this threat finally manifest itself? _____

   _____

6. How is the death of Gandiva worse to Arjun than his own death? _____

   _____

7. Regardless of what now happens to Arjun, how will his belief in destiny and sense of duty keep him going? _____

   _____

8. What do you predict will happen to Arjun in the final chapters? What will his *jati* or job become? Will he ever establish his Brahman birth status? Will he ever find his sister?

   _____

   _____

   _____

   _____

Friend or Foe?

In chapters 19 and 20 Arjun gains a new friend. He compares the aspects of his new friend with the other people he has met on his adventures. Look at the list of Arjun's friends and foes. Describe their personalities and what life-lessons Arjun learns from them.

Name	Friend or Foe?	Description and What Arjun Learned
Rama		
Gandiva		
Skanda		
Hari		
Vasu		
Manoja		

Make a list below of three of your friends. Describe the qualities you most admire in each friend and then explain how each of these friends has taught you to be a better person.

Name	Description	Lessons Learned
1. _____	_____	_____
	_____	_____
2. _____	_____	_____
	_____	_____
3. _____	_____	_____
	_____	_____

Write a New Ending

As the story closes, there are still a few unanswered questions about Arjun, his family, his duty, and his destiny. Imagine you are the author of this book. How would you conclude the story of Arjun's quest? Answer the following questions to help you formulate your ending.

1. Throughout the book there are many references to duty. From the beginning, Arjun dismisses his duty to his birth status of Brahman, and he does not follow his intended path to become a scholar or priest. This conflicts with the Hindu belief as stated in the *Bhagavad Gita*, "There is more joy in doing one's own duty badly than in doing another man's duty well." How would you explain Arjun's understanding of duty in this final chapter? _____

   _____

2. Another theme stated throughout the book is the quest for destiny. In chapter 20 Manoja tells Arjun as he is about to die, "You haven't found it yet. Where you should be . . . . You won't end here . . . . You got this far. It would be too strange if you go no further. Life is strange, but not that strange." What did Manoja mean by this?_____

   _____

   What do you feel is Arjun's final destiny? _____

   _____

   How does he find this destiny? _____

   _____

   What does he learn about himself and his destiny? _____

   _____

   What is his purpose in life? _____

   _____

3. At the end of the story, we have not learned about Arjun's sister or his family. What do you think happened to his sister?_____

   _____

   Does he ever find her? If so, how?_____

   _____

   Does Arjun ever attempt to make contact with his family again? Why or why not? _____

   _____

4. What does the future hold for Arjun? _____

   _____

   Where will your ending leave Arjun in his life? _____

   _____

Indian Vocabulary

Label a piece of paper for each of the categories below. Copy the words assigned by your teacher, or those you find as you read about India, and define each one.   Be as specific and detailed as possible. Add other words you find to the categories as you complete the unit. Many of these words can be used later to form an ABC Picture Book of India.

Social Structure
- artisan
- Brahmans
- caste system
- jati
- Kshatriyas
- panchamas
- Sudras
- Vaishyas
- varnas

Economy and Trade
- barter
- caravan
- Indus Valley Seal
- Old Silk Road
- trade routes

Education
- Arabic-Hindu Numbers
- *Bhagavad-Gita*
- guru
- Mahabharata
- Sanskrit
- swami
- yogi

Daily Life
- banyan tree
- batik
- betel
- chapati bread
- citadel
- dhoti
- monsoon
- sari
- tilaki mark
- turban
- vegetarian

Religion
- Ajanta Caves
- Ancient India
- animal sacrifice
- Buddha
- Buddhism
- cremation
- dharma
- enlightened
- funeral pyre
- Hinduism
- kapalikas
- karma
- lila
- meditation
- moksha
- Muslim
- nirvana
- offering
- pilgrimage
- polytheism
- reincarnation
- ritual
- sati
- shrine
- Sikhs
- *Veda*
- yoga

Government/Military
- Aryans
- gaja
- Gupta Empire
- harem
- Indus Valley Civilization
- Maharajah
- mahout
- Mauryan Empire
- Mogul Empire
- Sultan

A Classroom *Rig-Veda*

Historians know about the Aryan religion from four collections of poems and hymns called the *Veda*. Priests recited these hymns at sacrifices and ceremonies. Some of the poems were addressed to specific gods, while others described battles, observations, and dialogues. Because there was no written language, these poems and hymns were memorized and passed down orally. It was not until centuries later that the hymns were recorded in Sanskrit. The *Rig-Veda*, which contains 1,028 poems and hymns, remains one of India's most sacred Hindu texts, much like the Hebrew *Torah* and Christian *Bible*. Some of the hymns are still sung at weddings and funerals in modern India.

Below are some examples of hymns from the *Rig-Veda* that are dedicated to *Indra*, the god of the sky and weather, who rides through the heavens on his white elephant.

Indra, who wields the thunderbolt in his hand, is the king of that which moves and that which rests, of the tame and of the horned. He rules the people as their king, encircling all this as a rim encircles spokes.

He who made fast the tottering earth, who made still the quaking mountains, who measured out and extended the expanse of the air, who propped up the sky—he, my people, is Indra.

Activity:

Write a short poem that praises nature, family, school, friends, sports, or anything else that you feel is important in your life.

1. Write your poem on a piece of plain white paper, leaving a margin for binding.

2. Illustrate your poem with a colorful picture.

3. Work with classmates to assemble a book of the completed poems. If desired, organize the poems and hymns into chapters based on subject matter. Design a cover using a large sheet of colored construction paper. Punch holes and bind the book using brads.

5. Read the poems together as a class. Display your classroom *Rig-Veda* for future reading.

6. How is your book similar to the Hindu *Rig-Veda*? How is it different? How long do you think it would take to memorize all of the poems if you could not read them? How long do you think it took a young Aryan priest to memorize all 1,028 hymns of the *Rig-Veda*?

Above all is family, the tie that binds our love together.

Praise our union.

Praise our patience.

Praise our happiness.

Comparing Life Stages

In ancient India a person's life was divided into four main stages, each marked by rituals and ceremonies. Some basic information about life stages in ancient India is provided on the chart below. Research to learn more about these different stages of life and the associated rituals. Complete the chart by recording information about life stages in our modern society.

Use the completed chart to write an essay comparing life in our society today with that in ancient India. How are our observations of life milestones similar? How are they different? Begin with an introduction that gives some interesting background information to introduce the topic and explains the two subjects being compared, marking the life stages in ancient India and today. End with a conclusion that summarizes your points and gives a strong closing statement.

Ancient India	Life Stages	Modern Society
Rituals: birth/naming ceremony, astrological sign, celebration for every new achievement Joyous and innocent	**Childhood**	
Ritual: (males) an initiation ceremony, "twice born" males received thread. **Male:** disciplined in mind and body, study with guru **Female:** no formal schooling or ritual, prepare for marriage	**Student life**	
Ritual: marriage ceremony with family and friends Arranged marriage to own jati and caste. No divorce is allowed. The father has say over entire family, even after children leave home.	**Marriage and family**	
Ritual: none Simplicity and renouncement of material things. One gains respect and authority by retreating to lead a spiritual life in preparation for death and reincarnation.	**Old age**	

Indian Myths and Tales

Like all cultures, ancient Indians wrote many legends and myths to help explain the world around them. The following is a version of "The Descent of the Ganges," which explains how the sacred Ganges River came to be on Earth:

> *Long ago a humble and holy hermit wished to honor his dead ancestors by sprinkling their ashes into the sacred Ganges River. He made the long pilgrimage to northeastern India, but lo and behold the land sat barren of water. Rather than returning home disappointed, he turned his head to the skies and pleaded with the gods.*

> *The goddess Ganges lived above in her heavenly realm, stubborn and vain, refusing to come down to Earth. The hermit was determined to win her favor and convince her to send her waters flowing. To show his faith and sincerity, he raised his arms up to the sky and balanced on one foot. Days went by. Then weeks and months, but the hermit stood fast in his pose. Several years passed, and the hermit grew weak from hunger and lack of movement. His body shriveled and his beard touched the ground.*

> *Finally, as he began to take his last breaths, Lord Shiva was moved. He commanded the goddess Ganges to grant the faithful hermit his wish to sanctify his ancestors. Ganges protested and threatened to flood the entire earth. Just as she began her immense flow from heaven, Shiva leaped into the stream of water forcing the flow through his twisted locks of hair. Water gently poured down from the heavens and created the many tributaries of the Ganges River. Creatures big and small gathered to thank Lord Shiva for his divine mercy. The world was saved from destruction once again.*

Other Indian tales come from the Hindu *Panchatantra*, a collection of tales and sayings used to teach children how to act wisely. The following is a famous *Panchatantra* proverb: "The firefly seems a fire, the sky looks flat; Yet sky and fly are neither this nor that." Buddha also used tales and stories, called *Jakata Tales*, to teach his followers lessons. In each of the stories the main characters learn the importance of loyalty, honor, humility, peace, generosity, love, charity, or faith. *Panchatantra* and *Jakata Tales* are much like *Aesop's Fables*.

Write Your Own Indian Tale:

1. Read some other Indian tales from your local library. See page 79 for suggested titles. Look for characteristics that are common to all of the stories, like magic, involvement of Hindu gods in Hindu tales, reference to Indian culture, names, places, clothing, food, animals, plants, etc.

2. Decide whether you are going to write a myth that explains a natural phenomenon like "The Descent of the Ganges," or a story that teaches a lesson like the *Panchatantra* or the *Jakata Tales*.

3. Use the Story Plot Outline on page 45 to organize your story. Try to include as many references to Indian culture as possible. Write a rough draft. Have a partner review your draft and help revise both content and grammar. Write a final draft. Include illustrations to enhance your story.

4. If desired, combine your story with those of your classmates to create a class book of Indian tales.

Indian Myths and Tales *(cont.)*

Story Plot Outline

I. Introduction

A. Character descriptions_____

_____

B. Setting descriptions_____

_____

C. Problems or conflicts to be resolved by the end _____

_____

II. Plot—Sequence of Events

A. Obstacles/scenes leading to the climax

1. _____

_____

2. _____

_____

3. _____

_____

B. Climax—the scene where the problem is solved—peak of excitement_____

_____

_____

_____

III. Conclusion/Resolution

_____

_____

_____

_____

Life of a Maharajah

Throughout India's history its kings and rulers have played important and colorful roles. Some were famous for their wisdom and courage in battle while others were noted for their magnificent palaces and displays of wealth. Imagine that you are a Maharajah in ancient India. Describe the following details about your reign, and then complete the writing and drawing activity at the bottom of the page.

Your name: _____

The name of your kingdom and its location in India: _____

_____

Your palace and throne: _____

_____

Your harem:_____

_____

Your wealth and jewels: _____

_____

Favorite leisure activities and lifestyle characteristics: _____

_____

What you are most noted for:_____

_____

What the people in your kingdom think of you: _____

_____

What other rulers and visiting foreigners think of you: _____

_____

Writing and Drawing Activity:

1. Use the above information to write a short autobiography on another piece of paper about your life as a Maharajah in ancient India. Be as detailed and specific as possible, using elaborate, figurative language to portray an exotic image of your reign.

2. After you have completed the autobiography, add details to the figure on the following page to create a colorful picture of yourself in full regal attire. In the background draw a picture of your palace. Next to you draw a picture of your harem, possessions, animals, people in your court, visitors, or whatever else you feel typifies your reign.

3. Staple your autobiography and picture onto a sheet of construction paper to display in the classroom. Share your writing and picture with others. What similarities do you find?

Life of a Maharajah *(cont.)*

Using pictures from resource books as a guide, add details to the figure to create a picture of yourself as a Maharajah in ancient India. Include a picture of your palace and other noble possessions or friends. Make the picture as detailed and colorful as possible.

The Hindu-Arabic Number System

The number system which we use today was developed in India by the Hindus. The system uses ten symbols and is a place value system based on powers of ten. Zero is used as a place holder. Unlike other number systems, or primitive tally marks, a place value system does not add the sum of the digits. Instead, each numeral has a different value depending on its place in the number. Each place has a value that is ten times larger than the place to its right. For example, the number 57,932 actually represents (5 x 10,000) + (7 x 1,000) + (9 x 100) + (3 x 10) + (2 x 1). A place-value chart would look like this:

1,000,000's	100,000's	10,000's	1,000's	100's	10's	1's
10 x 100,000	10 x 10,000	10 x 1,000	10 x 100	10 x 10	10 x 1	1 x 1

Around 2,000 years ago when the system was first developed, the number symbols looked a bit different than they do today. The original Hindu numbers did not have a symbol for zero, but instead used special symbols for 10, 20, 30, 40, 50, 60, 70, 80, 90, 100, and 1,000. To write a number like 5,792 they would write 5 and the symbol for 1,000, then 7 and the symbol for 100, then the symbols for 90 and 2. In the fifth century the Hindus invented the concept of zero, and this revolutionary concept led to the place value system we use today, the decimal system. The new system, using zero, proved to be superior to other number systems because it required fewer symbols and made computation easier. Eventually, the Arabs adopted the system and carried it with them throughout Europe on their trading missions. The new number system replaced Roman numerals in the Western world, and the symbols were called Hindu-Arabic numerals. Although the individual number symbols changed slightly over time, with the invention of the printing press, they became standardized. This system was so superior that it is still used today.

Activity:

1. Write the number 247 using tally marks and Roman numerals. How is the Hindu-Arabic number system easier? _____

_____

2. Add 25 + 47 using tally marks and Roman numerals. How is the Hindu-Arabic number system easier? _____

_____

The Hindu-Arabic Number System *(cont.)*

The Hindu-Arabic number system is called the decimal system today because it is a base-ten place-value system. Fill in the missing parts to the place-value chart below.

hundred millions		millions	hundred-thousands		thousands	hundreds	tens	ones
	10,000,000s (10 x 1,000,000)		10,000s (10 x 1,000)			100s (10 x 10)	10s (10 x 1)	1s (1 x 1)

Read the words and write the correct corresponding Hindu-Arabic or decimal system number.

1. Two hundred sixteen thousand, five hundred fifty _____

2. Four hundred two thousand, nineteen _____

3. Ten million, twelve thousand, forty-five _____

4. Five hundred fifty million, five hundred six thousand, five _____

5. Two billion, three hundred fifty-two million, eighty-five thousand, six hundred eight

　_____

Tell the actual value the given symbol represents in each numeral below.

6. In 2,598,678,058 the 5 represents_____and_____.

7. In 56,243,298 the 2 represents_____and_____.

8. In 657,897,403,006 the 7 represents_____and_____.

Directions For Playing Highest Number:

1. Prepare a set of Hindu Arabic number cards by cutting ten 3" x 5" (7.6 cm x 12.7 cm) index cards in half and writing each digit from 0–9 on a card.

2. Place the digits face down on a desk and mix them up.

3. Draw one card at a time, lining them up on your desk to make a number. The first card will be in the billions place, the second card the hundred millions place, the third card the ten millions place, etc., until you have filled each place to the ones.

4. Write the number on a sheet of paper using Hindu-Arabic numbers. and then write the number in words.

5. The winner is the person with the highest number written correctly in both numbers and words.

Answer Key (*Cover before copying*): 1. 216,550 2. 402,019 3. 10,012,045 4. 550,506,005 5. 2,352,085,608
6. 500,000,000 and 50 7. 200,000 and 200 8. 7,000,000,000 and 7,000,000

Indus Valley Weights and Measures

Much evidence has been found to show that the Indus Valley had extensive trade routes throughout Mesopotamia and the Persian Gulf. Stone weights cut precisely into cubes give further evidence of trade and accounting. These weights varied in size to measure items from small amounts of gold to bushels of wheat. Some of the weights were so heavy that ropes were required to lift them. Try your hand at measuring and estimating using the Indus Valley weight system. Follow the directions below to hold a contest with classmates. The person with the lowest score wins!

Materials: Cube shaped objects of equal mass to use as the standard weights (Unifix cubes, small wooden blocks, base 10 blocks, sugar cubes, etc.), five balance scales, copies of the chart below for each student, five small objects like a pencil, a marker, a roll of tape, a tennis ball, and a ruler for estimating and weighing)

Directions:

1. Divide the class into five groups. Provide weights and a balance scale for each group. Give one of the objects to be estimated and weighed to each group.

2. The object of the activity is to predict the weight of each item as accurately as possible. To begin the activity, each person in the group holds the item to be weighed in his or her hand. Next, each holds the weights and predicts how many cubes will equal the item. (The predictions should be kept secret from the other members of the group.)

3. After each member of the group records his or her prediction on his or her chart, work as a group to weigh the object using the balance scale and the cube-shaped weights. Record the actual weight on the charts. Calculate individual scores by finding the difference between the predicted weight and the actual weight. Record the scores on the chart.

4. Rotate items among the groups until all groups have predicted and weighed each item. Calculate the final scores by adding all of the numbers in the score column. A low score indicates that you would make an excellent merchant or trader. If you have a high score, you should stick to pushing a plow! The winner is the person with the lowest score.

Weights and Measures Chart

Item	Predicted weight in cubes	Actual weight in cubes	Score (differences)
1.			
2.			
3.			
4.			
5.			

Total score_____

Make a Map of India

Use an atlas to find and label all of the geographical features listed in the box. Color the mountains yellow and all water and rivers blue. Color neighboring countries red.

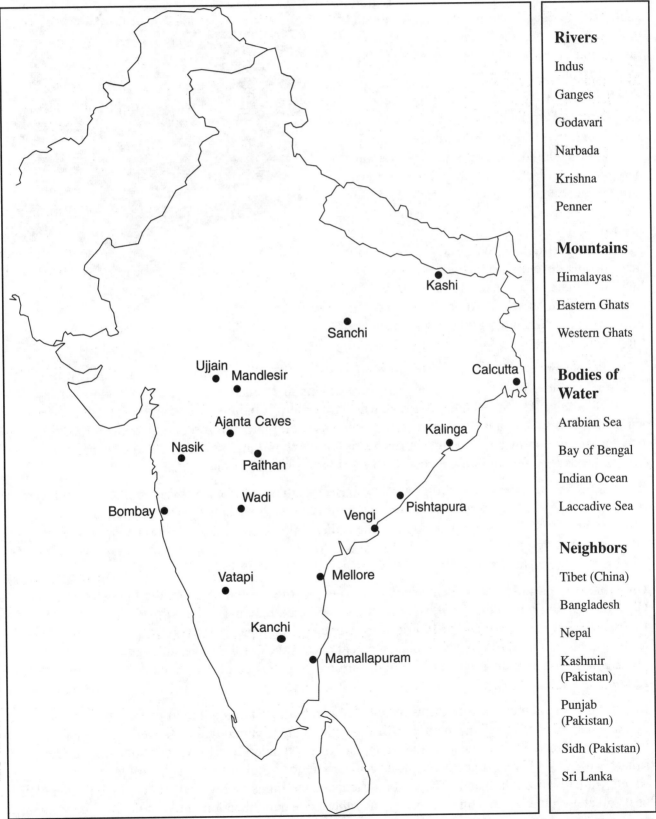

Rivers

Indus

Ganges

Godavari

Narbada

Krishna

Penner

Mountains

Himalayas

Eastern Ghats

Western Ghats

Bodies of Water

Arabian Sea

Bay of Bengal

Indian Ocean

Laccadive Sea

Neighbors

Tibet (China)

Bangladesh

Nepal

Kashmir (Pakistan)

Punjab (Pakistan)

Sidh (Pakistan)

Sri Lanka

The Indus Valley Civilization

India's earliest known civilization originated on the fertile flood plains of the Indus River in northwestern India. The climate of this region in ancient times was much like it is today, hot and dry. Although only the lower valley receives much rainfall during the monsoon season, the monsoon rains cause the river to flood, creating rich deposits of silt for farming crops of wheat, barley, dates, and melons.

Around 5,000 B.C. primitive farmers began settling in scattered villages in the hilly region near the river. Each season they traveled down into the valley and cultivated the rich soil left by the river floods. They could not live in the valley itself because they could not protect their homes against the destructive flood waters. Eventually these people developed a technique to bake building bricks in an oven. Because these bricks were stronger than sun-dried bricks, people could move closer to the fertile grounds without fear of the floods.

With this discovery and migration into the valley, the civilization flourished. The farmlands were plentiful, the river supplied abundant water for drinking and irrigation, fish for food, and highways for travel and trade. The surrounding forests provided timber for building, fuel, and plentiful game animals. With such bountiful resources, larger towns soon grew, and some individuals turned to occupations like weaving, tanning leather, making pottery, or building furniture. The demand for luxury goods required cloth-dyers, bead makers, goldsmiths, and stone-cutters.

By about 2300 B.C. the towns had grown into bustling cities. Elaborate governmental systems were designed to keep order, a writing system was developed, religious beliefs emerged, and advances were made in other technical and artistic skills. The Indus Valley Civilization grew to be larger than any other ancient empire, including those of Egypt and Mesopotamia. Its two great centers were the cities of Mohenjo-Daro and Harappa.

Until the early part of the twentieth century, few people knew anything about the Indus Valley Civilization. Only mounds of dirt, some as high as 60 feet, remained where the great cities once flourished. Between 1856 and 1919 bricks from ancient Harappan roads and walls were carried away to be used in Indian railway beds. Archaeological excavations of the Indus cities began during the 1920s and 1930s, and the great cities were unearthed, revealing carefully planned and constructed city formats.

In the center of each city was a fortress or citadel which was raised on a mud-brick platform about 400 by 200 yards (364 m x 182 m) in size. This citadel and other public buildings were surrounded by very thick walls of baked brick. Outside the walls, the town extended for at least one square mile (2.6 square km). Both Harappa and Mohenjo-Daro were divided into large rectangular blocks by wide streets with advanced drainage. The sewer systems of the Indus Valley Civilization are considered one of its greatest achievements, unequaled by any other ancient civilization until the time of the Romans.

The Indus Valley Civilization *(cont.)*

By studying the artifacts at the various sites, we can learn about the everyday life of these ancient people, including their clothing, jewelry, games, weapons, and tools. Fragments of their written language have been found on small stone seals that were most likely used for identification, although they have yet to be deciphered. The seals do show, however, pictures of once native animals, gods, and scenes from religious legends. Although written records are unavailable, we can learn something about the ancient customs and ideas of this civilization from the physical remains of their cities. Because cities far from one another were consistent in town layout, sewage system, weights and measures, brick size, home construction, pottery style, religious articles, and jewelry designs, we can reason that this uniformity was due to extensive contacts between the cities. This type of contact usually indicates a well-administered, centralized government.

Archaeologists also note that there were very few changes in the 1,000 years that the civilization prospered. Objects found in the earliest settlements are almost identical to objects found in the latest settlements. This also indicates that the government must have been strong throughout the centuries. Curiously, the few weapons that have been found are poorly constructed, owing to the fact that the inhabitants had not discovered iron. Apparently, the rulers of this great civilization did not rely on force to achieve strict obedience from their people. Perhaps religious and cultural beliefs held them together as a nation. If this is true, it may explain the great continuity of Indian culture that extends even to this day.

Scholars believe that this great civilization disintegrated about 2,000 B.C. and have suggested several theories for its decline. The Indus people may have overgrazed their lands and cut down too many trees for fuel and building projects, leading to smaller harvests and a decrease in trade. In addition, they may have disrupted the natural habitat of native animals. Today the land around the Indus River is barren of forests and large game. Flooding or insufficient flooding of the river during a planting season may have caused a famine. Some of the Indus people may have migrated to other parts of India, like the Ganges River Valley, using their farming techniques to shift from wheat and grain cultivation to rice.

The idea of the Indus Valley people migrating into other areas of India may help to explain the great continuity in Indian culture. Although the fate of these people will never be known for certain, there is much evidence that many of their ideas and customs never entirely perished. Chickens were first domesticated for use as a food source in the Indus Valley. Toys used in towns along the Arabian Sea are practically identical to those unearthed in ancient Harappa. The bangles worn by Harappan women on wrists and ankles, as well as necklaces and earrings, are still fashionable in India today. Pictures show that pigtails were a popular hairstyle among Harappan women, and they remain the most common hairstyle among Indian women today. The Indus Valley people began spinning and weaving cotton cloth about 2,000 B.C.. Today cotton textiles are an important industry in India.

The Indus Valley Civilization *(cont.)*

The ancient Indus Valley people also appear to have had an influence on Hinduism. A great public bath excavated at Mohenjo-Daro resembles the large public baths found today adjoining many Hindu temples. Like modern Hindus, the Indus Valley people seemed to have had a strong belief in the purifying powers of water. Other connections to the Hindu religion include figures of gods and goddesses found in the ancient ruins that resemble images worshipped today. Sacred animals, such as the bull, played an important part in the ancient religion, just as in modern Hinduism. One stone carving found at Harappa shows a religious figure sitting with his legs folded in precisely the same manner as Hindu holy men sit today.

These ancient people also had an influence on the development of Indian art. Many of the patterns and designs found on Indus Valley pottery and seals appear centuries later on Indian temples and in paintings. The portrayal of lifelike animals is a skill also passed down by Indian artists.

Around 1500 B.C. bands of semi-nomadic people called Aryans began to migrate from what is now known as Iran into the Indus Valley region. Their weapons were superior, and they brought riding horses and chariots. They had ox-drawn wagons and cattle which served as a portable food supply, an advantage over the settled agricultural people of the region. The remaining Indus Valley people were no match for these invaders. Ancient legends recorded by Aryans centuries later tell of battles between the Aryans and a dark skinned people they called the Dasyus. Although there is no way to know for certain that the Dasyus were in fact the Indus Valley people, there is some evidence that the Indus Valley Civilization ended in violence. Skeletons at Mohenjo-Daro were found huddled together in protection, and burn marks on bricks suggest the town was set ablaze.

Questions and Activities:

1. Why did these ancient people choose to settle in this region? What benefits did it offer?

2. What invention allowed the people to move into the valley? How might fuel for this invention have caused the civilization's downfall?

3. How do archaeologists know that the civilization had a strong central government? Give two examples.

4. What were some of the technical advances of this society in architecture and city planning?

5. Name at least three examples of modern day objects or customs in India that are similar to ancient times.

6. Based on the information presented, what do you think happened to the Indus Valley Civilization? Support your theory with evidence from the passage.

7. Make two bricks out of clay. Let one dry in the sun and bake the other in a kiln or oven. Which brick withstands water the best? Which brick is harder to crack? What benefits does baking the brick have for building homes or walls?

Hindu Beliefs and Practices

Hinduism is one of the oldest religions in the world. Unlike many other religions, Hinduism does not have one main founder or leader. Indians call it *Sanatana Dharma*, the faith with no beginning and no end. The Aryans, who began moving into India about 1500 B.C., practiced *polytheism*, or the worship of many gods. They believed that different deities controlled different parts of nature, and they offered sacrifices to the gods in order to please them. The priests responsible for rituals and sacrifices were important members of Aryan society. The Aryans tolerated the beliefs of the native Indus Valley people, and eventually elements from the two religions blended in to a new belief system, Hinduism.

Much of the information about the ancient Aryan religion and the origins of Hinduism comes from sacred Hindu texts, called *Vedas*. The *Rig-Veda*, a series of hymns and poems recited by the early Hindu priests, is believed to date to about 1300 B.C.. The different Vedas have special religious meaning to the Hindus, much like the verses in the *Bible* and *Torah* have special meaning to Christians and Jews.

Legends were also created to simplify the religion's philosophy for the common man. The *Puranas*, the *Rumayana*, and the *Mahabharata* are all stories that teach Hindu values. These legends advocate the pursuit of four goals: righteous living, wealth and prosperity, love and happiness, and an end to the cycle of birth and death. Through these stories Hindus learn the essence of their religion.

To a Westerner, Hinduism can be confusing because instead of prescribing a set of rules for all to follow, Hinduism reveals profound "truths" about life and suggests various paths of righteous living. Each Hindu chooses the path that best fits his or her life, which gods to worship, and which rituals to follow. An emotional person is free to choose the path of love and devotion, while an intellectual might follow a path of mental discipline, and those who believe that "work is worship" may select the path of selfless service.

Three interlocking elements of belief are central to Hinduism: reincarnation, karma, and the law of *dharma*. Hindus believe that life is a ceaseless cycle of events with no beginning or end. Death and birth are both just phases in the cycle. Each person is reincarnated (reborn) repeatedly, until he or she reaches the final supreme goal of Absolute, called *Moksha*, by overcoming all evils and all earthly desires. Only then is the soul released from the cycle, never to be reincarnated again.

This concept is tied to *karma*, the belief that everything a person does has a consequence. Both good and bad deeds have an effect on a person's happiness or misery in their present life, as well as in future lives. Whether one reappears in the next life as a plant, an animal, a wealthy nobleman, or a servant depends on actions performed in previous lives.

The third main concept is that of *dharma*, or the belief that one is born into a particular station in life and it is his or her moral duty to live according to that station. Hindus feel that they should go about their daily lives without question or complaint, fulfilling their duties to society at their particular social level. If they perform their duties well, they will be rewarded by being born at a higher social level in the next life. However, if they do poorly, they will be punished with a lower station in life in their next incarnation.

Hindu Gods Identity Cards

Hindus can choose which gods to worship in order to reach the Absolute. Use resources on Hinduism to match the names of these Hindu Gods to their following descriptions and pictures. Add other information that you find in your resource materials to the cards. Color the cards, cut them apart, and staple them together to form a book. Keep this book handy as a reference throughout the unit.

Names of the Hindu Gods

a. Lord Shiva (Siva)   d. Lord Vishnu   g. Lord Brahma   j. Parvati

b. Durga (Devi)   e. Indra   h. Ganesha (Ganapati) k. Krishna

c. Surya (Savitr)   f. Agni   i. Ganga

---

1. _____ _____

The eldest son of Brahma, he is the god of fire and is colored red.

His fire links heaven and Earth by carrying people's sacrifices to the gods. His favorite pet is a ram.

---

2. _____ _____

This son of Shiva and Parvati has the head and body of an elephant. He is the patron of schools and letters. He is the god of learning and is worshipped at the start of any enterprise. He is also the god who wards off evil. He rode on a mouse that could gnaw through any obstacle.

---

3. _____ _____

He is called the Indestructible, the Creator of the World, the Supreme Ruler, and the Source of all Knowledge. He has four heads and is colored red. He rides on a swan or goose which symbolizes knowledge. In his four hands he holds a scepter, a ladle, beads, a bow, and a jug. He is part of the Hindu Trinity.

Hindu Gods Identity Cards *(cont.)*

4. ___ _____

This god is one of the incarnations of Vishnu on Earth.
He is the god featured in the Bhagavad-Gita and guides
the faithful from evil, reminding them of their duties. He is
colored blue and his name means "the dark one."

5. ___ _____

Known as the Destroyer, this god with twisted locks of hair
danced to destroy the universe so it could be reborn. He
often rides a bull, the symbol of victory. He has four arms
and his symbols are the ax and the drum. He is part of
the Hindu Trinity.

6. ___ _____

This god of sky, rain, thunder, and war rides a white
elephant named Airavata. He is one of the original Aryan
gods central to the *Rig-Veda*.

7. ___ _____

This river goddess personifies the Ganges River. She is
beloved by Shiva. Legend claims she came to Earth
through the twisted strands of Shiva's hair so she would
not flood the Earth.

Hindu Gods Identity Cards *(cont.)*

8. ____ _____

Known as the Preserver and the King of Serpents, this god rides on Ananta, the cosmic snake. His four arms represent pleasure, success, righteousness, and liberation, and in his four hands he holds a conch shell, a wheel, a mace, and a lotus. He has come to Earth in many animal and human forms. He is colored black or dark blue with a yellow veil at the hips. He is part of the Hindu Trinity.

9. ____ _____

Created by Vishnu and Shiva, this goddess rode out of the mountains on a red lion and defeated the king anti-god who was a buffalo, the symbol of death. She restored heaven to the gods and is considered the goddess of war, birth, and death.

10. ____ _____

This sun god rides his chariot, which has only one wheel and is drawn by seven golden horses, on a lotus.

11. ____ _____

This goddess is the daughter of the mountain and the wife of Lord Shiva. She is the mother of many gods and chief of all the elves and spirits who wander about the earth.

Comparing India's Main Religions

Teaching the lesson

1. Enlarge and copy the chart below on a chalkboard, bulletin board, or overhead projector to compare and contrast the features of some of India's main religions.

	Hinduism	Islam	Christianity	Sikhism	Buddhism	Jainism
Founder and/or leader						
Origins—how it began						
Deities (gods)						
Beliefs about death, afterlife, and reincarnation						
Roles of karma (fate) and dharma (conduct)						
Rules and requirements for followers						
Rituals or ways to worship						
Sacred texts						

2. Read the following passage to the class and tell the students that they will be comparing the features of India's major religions.

   As you have learned, India is a melting pot where many different migrant people came together to live, work, and worship. Two of the world's foremost religions, Hinduism and Buddhism, were founded in India, along with the two uniquely Indian religions, Jainism and Sikhism. Islam and Christianity were brought to India by conquerors and missionaries and have become important minority religions.

   Today, over 80 percent of India's 950 million people are Hindus. There are also over 100 million Muslims, 20 million Christians, 18 million Sikhs, 7.5 million Buddhists, 4 million Jains, and countless followers of other faiths. Religion plays an important part in the life of Indians on the whole. Almost every joyous occasion is celebrated with a visit to a shrine, temple, mosque, or church. Virtually every day of the year marks a festive occasion associated with one faith or another. Assimilation of these various religious values have made the people of India generally very tolerant. However, religious unrest is not uncommon, especially in recent years when politicians have exploited religious differences.

3. Divide the class into six groups and assign one of the religions to each group. Make sure each group understands the different categories for research and has an adequate supply of resource materials from this unit, as well as other books from the library.

4. After each group has completed its research, have the students prepare a brief presentation and record their information on the classroom chart. Each student in the group should be responsible for a portion of the presentation.

5. Discuss the similarities and differences between the religions. What can we learn from India about freedom of religion? Why do you feel Hinduism has remained dominant for so many years despite the influx of so many other religions?

Trade Route Map

Early traders were dazzled by the variety and quality of goods they found in India. Extensive trade routes developed to carry the spectacular goods from India to the West. After traveling across the Arabian Sea using the monsoon winds, traders sailed up the Red Sea and Persian Gulf to reach Mesopotamia and Egypt. They then crossed overland to sail across the Mediterranean and trade with Northern Africa, Greece, and Rome. To the East, India traded with China, Southeast Asia, and Indonesia. Early trade routes were controlled by the Arabs but later Europeans joined the trade boom.

During the first century A.D., Indian trade with Rome flourished. Luxury goods, such as gems, precious stones, pearls, ivory, and perfumes, were exported to wealthy Roman wives along with special spices including pepper, ginger, and cinnamon. The famous Roman toga required finely woven cotton cloth, as well as red and indigo dyes from India. Timber such as Indian teak and ebony were in great demand for furniture. Thousands of elephants, tigers, lions, and water buffalo were exported from India to perform in the lavish and bloodthirsty Colosseum spectacles. Smaller animals like monkeys, parrots, and peacocks were traded as pets. Lesser exports included rice, sugar, iron, and leather goods.

The Romans paid for these goods in tons of gold. Roman coins have been discovered all over India, especially in the south near the main trading ports. Romans also bartered for goods using Roman pottery, glassware, tin, lead, coral, wine, and slave girls. India's other great imports of the time included silk from China and horses from the Arabian Peninsula and Asia.

Use the information above to draw the trade routes on the map. Answer the questions on the back of this page.

1. Draw a trade route going from China, along the eastern and western coast of India, and through the Persian Gulf. If these merchants set off on foot to the northwest, who would they trade with?

2. Draw a trade route from Calicut, across the Arabian Sea, up the Red Sea and into the Mediterranean. If you continue sailing west, what are three places you could stop to trade?

3. List at least five imports of India and the place where the goods originated.

4. By using the heavy monsoon winds, traders could finally cross the Arabian Sea. Pretend you are a merchant on a sailing vessel. Describe your perilous journey during the monsoon season.

Design an Ancient Indian City

Imagine that you are a city planner for an ancient city in India. Use this page to plan, design, and write about your city.

1. What is the name of your city? _____

2. Where in India is it located? Use an atlas to find the latitude and longitude. Also give reference to major landmarks. For example: Patna is a city in northeastern India near the Ganges River. It is located at approximately 26° North and 85° East. _____

   _____

   _____

   _____

3. Draw a map of your ancient city on a large sheet of construction paper. Include the items below. Color and label the map clearly.

   - a citadel
   - homes for the wealthy
   - guilds for craftsmen
   - the granaries
   - a thick city wall made of brick
   - homes for workers

   - guilds for merchants
   - farmland and homes outside the wall
   - gates in the wall for access
   - public ponds and gardens
   - temples and public baths
   - network of roads with sewers

4. Describe the life in your city as if you were a travel agent or real estate broker. What is it like to live there? What would I see if I were walking down the streets? What sounds and smells are typical in your city? What do the people look like? What type of work is available? What places could I visit? What do people do for leisure?

   _____

   _____

   _____

   _____

   _____

   _____

   _____

   _____

   _____

   _____

Time Line of India

Work in small groups to create time lines of India using the following materials: 14 sheets of paper, scissors, glue, markers, tape, a copy of the list of events.

Directions:

1. Tape the 14 sheets of paper together to form your time line and label as shown:

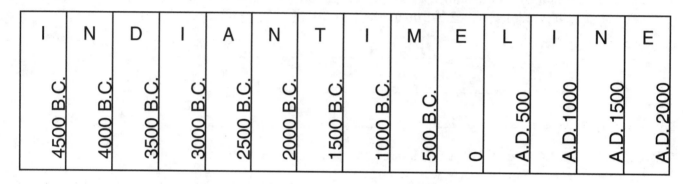

I	N	D	I	A	N	T	I	M	E	L	I	N	E
4500 B.C.	4000 B.C.	3500 B.C.	3000 B.C.	2500 B.C.	2000 B.C.	1500 B.C.	1000 B.C.	500 B.C.	0	A.D. 500	A.D. 1000	A.D. 1500	A.D. 2000

2. Write the following events and any others you have found in your study of India in the proper place on your time line.

3. Add colored pictures to different sections of the time line to enhance understanding.

Events

5000 B.C.   Farming has begun in western parts of India.

2500 B.C.   The Indus Valley Civilization is at its height.

2000 B.C.   The Indus Valley Civilization collapses for unknown reasons.

1500 B.C.   The Vedic age begins with the arrival of the Aryans in northwestern India.

563-483 B.C.   Life of Siddhartha Gautama who founds the Buddhist religion.

500s B.C.   The Persians invade northwestern India.

327 B.C.   Alexander the Great defeats the Persians and expands his Grecian Empire into northwestern India. Greek influence is found in Indian art and sculpture.

321 B.C.   Chandragupta Maurya founds the great Mauryan Empire in central India. With a Greek envoy he writes *Indika*, a detailed account of the Indian experience.

269 B.C.   Mauryan Empire is at its height under Asoka and covers most of India.

231 B.C.   Asoka dies, and the Mauryan Empire begins to crumble.

184 B.C.   The Mauryan Empire ends. India divides into a number of smaller kingdoms with no central government for the next 500 years.

100s B.C.   Arabs control the trade routes to and from India.

A.D. 50   Trade flourishes with the Roman Empire across the Mediterranean.

A.D. 100   Buddhism reaches China.

A.D. 300s   Rome begins to decline in power. Arabs regain control of the Indian trade routes.

Time Line of India *(cont.)*

A.D. 320	The Gupta Empire forms in the Ganges Valley and Magadha unifies India. Called the Golden Age of India, science and the arts flourish under Chandra Gupta II.
A.D. 399	Fa-Hsien travels across India to bring sacred Buddhist texts to China.
A.D. 500s	Huns threaten the Gupta Empire which eventually divides into smaller kingdoms.
A.D. 630-645	Hsuan Tsang makes a Buddhist pilgrimage across India. He is considered a hero when he returns to China with Buddhist texts.
A.D. 711	Arabs conquer Sind near the Indus River Delta. Islam filters into India.
A.D. 1001	Turk Mahmud of Ghazni from Afghanistan leads large scale Muslim invasions. He attempts to plunder the wealth of Hindu temples.
A.D. 1100	Turks establish the Delhi Sultanate Empire and rule the Ganges Valley until 1300. Raziya, the first woman ruler in the Muslim world, governs Delhi.
A.D. 1200	Muslim Turks of the Ganges Valley attempt an unsuccessful raid of southern India. Two independent southern kingdoms, the Muslim Bahmani and the Hindu Vijayanagar Kingdoms, fight constantly over fertile lands.
A.D. 1520	Vijayanagar Kingdom reaches its peak in southern India. There is increased trade with Portugal.
A.D. 1526	The Mogul Empire in northern India is founded by Babur.
A.D. 1556	Akbar, the greatest Mogul emperor, rules for almost 50 years. He strengthens the empire, reclaims lands and wins the loyalty of nobles and Hindus by practicing religious tolerance.
A.D. 1565	Southern India is conquered and ruled by Muslims. Most of India is controlled by the Mogul Empire who devise brilliant systems of administration and communication.
A.D. 1600s	Considered the Golden Age of the Mogul Empire, the luxurious palaces, thrones, and finery present a spectacle of wealth to visitors from Europe.
A.D. 1619	The English East India Company sets up a factory at Surat.
A.D. 1627	Shah Jahan's reign begins. He builds the Red Fort in Delhi, the Agra Fort, and the Taj Mahal as a memorial to his wife.
A.D. 1707	The death of the last great Mogul Emperor, Aurangzeb, weakens the Empire.
A.D. 1720	The French establish their first trading post at Pondicherry.
A.D. 1784	With the India Act, the British take political control of India.
A.D. 1799	Ranjit Singh rules over the Sikh kingdom of Punjab for 40 years.
A.D. 1857	The First War of Independence is fought.
A.D. 1876	Queen Victoria of England is proclaimed the empress of India.
A.D. 1885	The Indian National Congress is founded to help get Indian views heard in the English-run government. The goal is self-rule for India.
A.D. 1906	The all-Indian Muslim League, aimed at creating a separate state for Muslims, is founded. Eventually Pakistan breaks off from India as an all-Muslim state.
A.D. 1920	Mohandas Gandhi launches his campaign of civil disobedience to help gain India's independence.
A.D. 1947	India finally gains independence.
A.D. 1948	Mohandas Gandhi is assassinated.

Heart Beat Meditation

One of the meditation techniques practiced by both Hindus and Buddhists involves controlling breathing and thinking to reach a state of peacefulness. Some people are effective enough to control their heart rates as well. Work in groups of three to see how meditation affects breathing and heart rate by completing this experiment.

Purpose: The purpose of this experiment is to observe the effects of meditation on breathing and heart rate.

Materials: You will need the chart below and a stop watch.

Hypothesis: Meditation can be used to slow one's breathing and heart rate.

Procedure:

1. Have a friend find your pulse on your wrist. He or she will count the number of pulses, or heart beats, in one minute while another friend uses a stop watch to time the measurement. While your friends are timing your heart beats, count how many times you breathe during that minute. Breathe naturally without controlling your inhaling or exhaling.

2. Record your findings on the chart below.

3. Now do 25 jumping jacks. Repeat the procedure above, timing your breathing and pulse rate for one minute. The figures should be higher since exercise increases work to your body.

4. Record your findings on the chart below.

5. Wait about 5 minutes, or until you feel your heart rate is back to normal, then sit cross-legged on the floor, placing your hands palms up on your knees. Close your eyes and take slow deep breaths. (This part of the experiment will only work if you can be serious.) Think about slowing down your heart by relaxing and being calm. Picture a calm, soothing environment and try to block out anything happening around you. Allow at least 3 minutes of serious meditation before you begin timing. Concentrate on your slow, deep breathing while your partners time both your breathing and heart beats for one minute.

6. Record your findings on the chart below.

7. Change roles until all members of the group have tried the experiment.

Results

	Heart beats/minute	Breaths/minute
Starting Rate		
After Exercise		
After Meditation		

Conclusion: What did you learn about meditation? Were you able to slow your breathing and heart rate below your starting rate? If not, what factors do you think inhibited the experiment? Record your conclusions on the back of this paper.

Experiment with Indian Textiles

India is renowned for its cotton and silk textiles, created with batik and tie-dye processes. Experiment with dyes on cotton or silk fabric to discover the wonders of Indian textiles.

Materials:

Red, yellow, and blue fabric dyes (Look at a craft or drug store for dyes that work in warm to cool water.), pieces of cotton or silk cloth (pillow cases, T-shirts, socks, scarves, etc. of 100 percent cotton or silk, prewashed for best results), four large buckets or tubs, heavy duty rubber bands, rubber gloves, aprons or other protective clothing, newspaper.

Directions:

(Use newspapers, an old plastic tablecloth, or large plastic bags to protect the work surface.)

1. Follow the package instructions to make a dye bath of a different color in each tub. In the fourth tub, make a rinse of clear water.

2. Think about the design you want to create. Pleat, twist, or knot your fabric and tie it securely. The dye will not penetrate the knotted areas. Some examples are shown on the right.

3. Consider the way colors mix. For instance, yellow and red will make orange. You may wish to chart the possible combinations of the colors you will be using. Think about the combinations which will occur when you dye one color over another as you plan your design.

4. Now draw a picture on the back of this page to predict what your cloth will look like. Use crayons, colored pencils, or markers to show the colors and designs on the cloth.

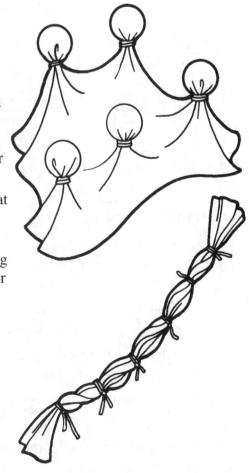

5. Wear rubber gloves, and, if desired, an apron when working with the dye. Beginning with the lightest color, place all or part of the knotted fabric into the dye bath. Leave it there for at least 5 minutes or until the dye is well absorbed.

6. Take it out and rinse it immediately in the cool water. Change the rinse water as needed.

7. Let it dry for a while, then place part of the cloth into another color of dye.

8. Rinse, dry, and repeat using the last color.

9. Untie the cloth and rinse it one last time in clear water.

10. Compare the finished cloth to your prediction. Was your prediction close? Why or why not? Draw a picture of your actual cloth on the back of this page. What did you learn about Indian textiles? Is tie-dyeing as easy as you thought it would be?

Make an Indus Valley Seal Print

One of the great discoveries in Harappa and Mohenjo Daro was the collection of stone seals. The seals were square, with markings and pictures of animals or gods. Have students recreate these seals and make prints using large index cards, brayers, and printing ink.

Preparing for the Lesson:

1. Gather examples of Indus Valley seals from books and magazines. Gather enough for students to use as examples at their desks.

2. Each student will need two 4 inch by 8 inch (10 cm x 20 cm) index unruled cards, scissors, and glue to make his or her seal.

3. You will need tubes of printing ink (Speedball is most commonly found at art or craft stores.), brayers to roll on the ink, foam meat trays to hold the ink, and colored construction paper on which to make the print.

4. Cover the table where you are going to do the printing with butcher paper, newspaper, or plastic. Provide a paper towel for each student.

5. Make one seal print yourself before teaching the lesson.

Finished Seal Print

#5

#8

Teaching the Lesson:

1. Tell the students that they are going to make their own Indus Valley Seal prints using large index cards. Review the Indus Valley Civilization and show examples of different seals from resource materials.

2. Distribute the cards, scissors, and glue to the students. Have each student draw a design on one of the cards. Tell them to cut out their designs so that each detail is visible and cut out.

3. Have students cut their remaining cards into a square. Glue the pieces from the first card onto this square card. This is now their seal.

4. Allow the glue to dry completely.

5. Place the square seal faceup on a paper towel on the covered table. Squirt some printing ink onto the foam tray and spread it evenly over the brayer by rolling it back and forth in the tray.

6. Roll the ink covered brayer over the seal making sure all portions are covered with ink.

7. Turn the inked seal onto a sheet of contrasting construction paper. Rub the back of the seal to evenly transfer the ink to the paper.

8. Carefully peel the seal off of the construction paper to reveal the imprint. Trim edges and display.

Paint a Royal Elephant

One of the most revered animals in the Indian culture is the elephant. Elephants were used in battle, for transportation, and for status. Decorating elephants with fabric and chalk designs is still practiced today during major festivals. Have your students create a royal elephant of their own using charcoal and tempera paint.

Preparing for the lesson:

1. Gather pictures of elephants in profile, and, if possible, pictures of decorated elephants from India and the circus to be distributed to the students.

2. Each student will need a sheet of black construction paper, a watercolor paintbrush, and a charcoal chalk. Provide each student with scratch paper for practicing and cover the work areas with paper or plastic.

3. Students can work with partners to share paint trays and water cans. Make a paint tray using a foam egg carton. Place black, white, red, blue, green, yellow, and purple paint in the carton. Leave areas for mixing paint in the tray. Use a juice can, plastic tub, or tin can for water.

4. Make a sample elephant of your own before teaching the lesson.

Teaching the Lesson:

1. Discuss the use of elephants in ancient India. Tell students that they are going to paint their own royal elephant decorated in all its finery. Distribute the pictures of the elephants along with the scratch paper. Have students practice drawing outlines of their elephants. If desired, model for students on the chalkboard a basic elephant profile.

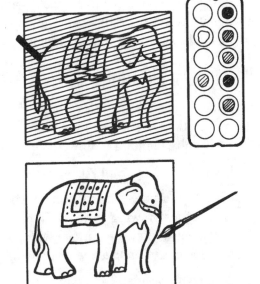

2. Once students have practiced the shape of their elephants, distribute the black construction paper and charcoal chalks. Have students use the black chalk to draw outlines of their elephants as large as possible on the black paper.

3. Next, have them add the other features and decorations. Remind the students that they will be painting the picture, so it is important to completely outline areas for different colors of paint.

4. Once the drawings are completed and you have checked them over, distribute the paints, paintbrushes, and water cans to partners. Since they are painting on black paper, they will need to mix white into the colors for them to show brightly. Have students experiment with mixing colors for the different features of their elephants. (If the paints are too thick to paint on smoothly, the students may dilute them with a bit of water.)

5. Have students paint their drawings, leaving a thick black line between the different sections. Choose a contrasting color to paint the entire background. Once the paintings are dry, display the herd of elephants around the classroom.

Sculpture and Cave Paintings

Indian Relief Sculptures

Relief sculptures, used to adorn public buildings and temples, were cut as projected images on a slab. You can make an Indian relief carving of your own using white tile grout, a deep foam tray, and simple carving tools such as a large nail, large paper clip, points of scissors, or a mechanical pencil without the lead.

1. Look for pictures of simple designs or figures used in carvings at Indian temples and buildings. *A Coloring Book of Ancient India* from Bellerophon Books is an excellent source.

2. Mix a batch of white tile grout with water so that you have enough to fill a deep foam tray at least 1 inch (3 cm) thick. (Tile grout is less expensive and less brittle than plaster of Paris.) Let the grout dry overnight.

3. Remove the slab of tile grout from the tray and draw a line around the outside edge indicating the depth of the carving. Use a sculpture tool, as mentioned above, to etch the design you will carve on the surface.

4. Carve away the background to the depth-line so that the design stands out from the background. Carefully etch details onto the design using a fine sculpting tool. If desired, paint your relief sculpture with watercolor paints.

Ajanta Cave Paintings

One of the greatest discoveries from ancient India is the series of Buddhist caves around Ajanta. The walls and ceilings are painted with intricate pictures of Buddha and his followers. You can recreate these images by painting with watercolors on crumpled brown paper bags.

1. Look for examples of Ajanta art in books. The Bellerophon coloring book has several examples.

2. Cut off one side of a large brown shopping bag. Crumple it up and then smooth it out again to create your drawing surface. In pencil create a design with people, plants, or animals. Try to fill in the entire drawing surface with patterns and designs to enhance your drawing.

3. Trace over your entire picture using a fine line black permanent marker, like a Sharpie. (A nonpermanent pen will run when painted.) Add details so that your picture is as intricate as those found in the caves.

4. Paint your picture using watercolors, or color it with markers. Once it is dry, tear the edges to give it an antique look. Display the complete work in the classroom.

Make a Taj Mahal

The Taj Mahal stands on the west bank of the Yamuna River near Agra. Building began in 1632 and took about 20 years to complete. It is built of white marble and was originally decorated with precious stones. Inside are the tombs of Momtaz Mahal and Shah Jahan. It is a fabulous feat of architecture which you can duplicate by following these directions:

1. Turn the outline of the Taj Mahal over and trace over the lines on the back using a fine line black marker. Add any designs and features that you want so that the building is covered with patterns like the original Taj Mahal.

2. Use colored pencils to add shading to the picture in yellows, browns, and pinks. Cut out your building and glue it to a sheet of black construction paper.

3. Display your Taj Mahal with the others from the class.

ABC Picture Book of India

As a culminating project to the unit, have your students make an alphabet picture book using words from India. The books can be made from large white index cards or sheets of construction paper. Have the students write the letters and words in bold lettering. Include a definition of the word and a colorful picture on each page. An example of a page, as well as suggested words for each letter, have been provided.

A　Ajanta Caves, Aryans, Asoka, astronomy

B　Brahmans, Buddha, Bay of Bengal, Bombay, Lord Brahma

C　Chalukyans, caste system, Calcutta

D　dhoti, dharma, Deccan Plateau, Delhi, Durga the goddess

E　evil spirits, Eight-fold Path, English Rule, enlightenment

F　Four Noble Truths

G　gaja, Gupta Empire, Ganapati (ganesha), Ganges Rivers, Gandhi (Mohandas)

H　Hinduism, harem, Himalaya Mountains

I　Indus Valley Civilization, Indra, Islam, Independence

J　jati, *Jakata Tales*, Jahangir the Mogul, Jesuits

K　Kshatriyas, kapalikas, Kalidasa the Poet, karma

L　lily, Lord Mountbatten, languages of India, legends of India, lion capital of Asoka

M　monsoon, mahout, Mauryan Empire, Mahabharata, meditation, moguls, Maharajah, monk

N　Narmada River, numbers (Arabic-Hindu), nirvana

O　Old Silk Road, oral tradition of learning the *Veda*

P　Panchamas, pranayama, purdah, Punjab, Parvati

Q　question of duty and destiny, questions by guru

R　*Rig-Veda*, rasa, reincarnation

S　Sudra, Sanskrit, Shiva, sati, Sikhs, sari

T　turban, tilaki mark, Taj Mahal

U　union territory, United Provinces

V　varnas, Vaishyas, Vishnu, Veda

W　weights and measures of Indus Valley Civilization

X　extraordinary temples, buildings, and monuments of India

Y　yoga, yogi

Z　zero concept

B　Buddhism

A religion of central and eastern Asia founded by Siddartha Gautama, the Buddha, in India, about 500 B.C. It teaches that right living and right thinking will enable the soul to reach nirvana, a divine state of release from early pain and desire.

Caste System Dramas

As a culminating activity to the unit, have students perform skits to illustrate the Indian caste system and how it worked in everyday life in ancient India.

1. Reproduce and review the information of the Indian Caste System, making sure students understand the rights and roles of the different classes.

2. Divide the class into five groups. Randomly assign each group with a class: The priests and scholars, or Brahmans; the Rajahs and warriors called Kshatriyas; the merchants and farmers called Vaishyas; the servants or Sudras; and the outcast untouchables called Panchamas.

3. Have each group use the available resources to research and record a set of rules that would have governed their class in ancient Indian society. Encourage them to write down specific behaviors toward other people in other classes. Have them select jobs, or jati, that would have been appropriate for their class in ancient India.

4. Once each group has completed its research and recorded all information, regroup the students. Each new group should have at least five members, one member from each of the classes.

5. Write the following situations on a chalkboard or overhead projector:

   A. A trip to the market   E. Traveling to visit relatives in a nearby city

   B. A religious festival   F. Joining a trading caravan

   C. Attending a cremation ceremony   G. Visiting a local temple to make offerings

   D. Going on a hunting excursion   H. A trip from the city to the countryside

6. Have each group select a situation in order to make up a short skit. The skit should illustrate how members of each of the classes interact with each other in the given situation. Each of the actors must adhere strictly to his or her own class rules during the performance.

7. After each performance, discuss the authenticity of the skit and how the classes treated and related to each other.

8. How is this different in India today? How are things still very much the same? How are the classes in our country similar or different? What does this tell you about equality and treating all people equally regardless of race, gender, religion, or economic class?

A Day in Ancient India

With the class, recreate a day in the life of the ancient Indians. Begin to plan for this day at least two weeks in advance. You may wish to team with another class or an entire grade level to share in this special day. Parents may also enjoy participating in all or some of the activities. After you have decided on a schedule of events, you may wish to write a letter to parents inviting them to participate.

Suggested Activities:

1. Encourage students to dress as Indians for the day. At least a week before the event, display pictures of typical Indian attire, and demonstrate wrapping a *sari* and *culottes*, as shown on pages 75 and 76. Discuss the suggested alternatives (you may wish to assemble one or more to illustrate). Give each student a copy of the appropriate page to take home as a reference.

2. Ask the students to bring food items to create an Indian feast. If you will be cooking part or all of the feast as a class activity, assign ingredients to be brought from home. If students will be preparing the dishes at home, provide copies of the recipes on pages 73 and 74. Schedule the feast near or in place of the lunch period. Provide cushions for seating and Indian music during the feast. Use plastic utensils and paper plates, napkins, and cups.

   ### Suggested Menu:

   Students may cook in class or bring dishes made at home. Use the following recipes on pages 73 and 74 or the substitutes listed in parenthesis below. Or check with a local Indian restaurant about providing a low cost meal in exchange for good advertising. The following can be served at your feast: fruit juice and herbal tea (Jasmine tea, if possible), *Raita*, a spice banana yogurt (fruit yogurt mixed with chunks of banana), *Pulao*, a spiced Basmati rice (packages of spiced Basmati rice), *Gajar Nariyal*, a carrot dish (raw carrot sticks and raisins), and *Chapatis*, unleavened bread (whole wheat tortillas).

3. Adorn the classroom with incense, cushions, and strands of paper flowers (see directions below). Display books and art created by the students.

4. Have groups of students perform Caste System Dramas (page 71) or reenact Panchatantra tales.

5. Create Indian artwork from pages 65–68.

6. Play an Indian game (page 77).

Decorating with strands of paper flowers:

Materials: white, yellow, and pink crepe paper, large embroidery needles, heavy thread

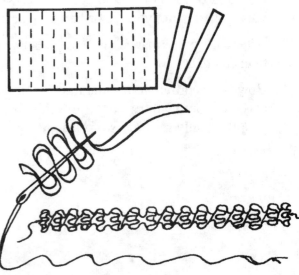

Directions: Using a paper cutter, cut the package of crepe paper into 1-inch (3 cm) wide strips. Thread the needle with a long piece of thread and knot the end. Begin stitching through the paper as shown. Push the paper down, expanding it and twisting it gently to give the illusion of a flower strand. Hang the strands throughout the room, connecting them as desired.

Recipes

Chapatis or Unleavened Whole Wheat Bread *(Makes 12–16 Chapatis)*

Ingredients

2 ½ cups (600 mL) whole wheat flour

2 tablespoons (30 mL) butter or margarine

1 teaspoon (5 mL) salt

1 cup (240 mL) lukewarm water

Directions:

(This recipe can be done the modern way with a large mixer having a dough hook or in the ancient tradition given in the directions)

1. Put 2 cups of the flour into a large mixing bowl.

2. Cut the butter into small pieces. Make a hollow in the center of the flour and add butter. Rub the butter into the flour with your fingertips until the mixture looks like large bread crumbs.

3. Mix the salt into the water. Add enough water, a little at a time, to the flour mixture to make a firm (but not stiff) dough.

4. Knead the dough in the bowl for about 5 minutes, and then cover with a damp cloth and let sit at room temperature for about 1 hour.

5. Divide and roll dough into pieces about the size of a walnut or golf ball.

6. Sprinkle the remaining flour on a flat surface for rolling out the dough. Using a rolling pin, roll out each ball until it resembles a flat pancake about ⅛ inch (.31 cm) thick.

7. On a greased griddle or skillet, cook each chapati until brown spots appear on the bottom and the edges curl up. Make sure you cook each side, turning it over with a spatula.

8. Wrap the cooked chapatis in a towel or foil to keep them warm. Serve warm with butter.

9. The chapatis may be deep fried.

Raita or Spicy Yogurt and Bananas *(Serves 12)*

Ingredients:

32 ounces (908g) plain yogurt

3 green chilies finely chopped

¾ teaspoon (3.75 mL) ground coriander

¾ teaspoon (3.75 mL) salt

6 large bananas peeled and sliced into chunks

3 teaspoons (15 mL) lemon juice

¾ teaspoon (3.75 mL) cinnamon

3 teaspoons (15 mL) finely chopped fresh coriander or cilantro leaves

Directions:

1. In a large mixing bowl, stir the yogurt until it is smooth. Stir in the bananas, chili, lemon juice, and spices.

2. Cover the bowl and chill at least 1 hour.

3. Just before serving, garnish with sprinkles of coriander leaves.

Recipes (cont.)

Pulao or Spiced Basmati Rice *(Serves 12–16)*

Ingredients:

²/₃ cup (160 mL) vegetable or peanut oil

1 medium onion, thinly sliced

1 teaspoon (5 mL) ground cloves

1 teaspoon (5 mL) cinnamon

1 teaspoon (5 mL) ground coriander

2 cups (480 mL) basmati or other long grain rice

4 cups (1 L) boiling water

1 teaspoon (5 mL) salt

2 tablespoons (30 mL) butter or margarine

¹/₂ cup (120 mL) raisins

4 tablespoons (60 mL) blanched slivered almonds or cashews

Directions

1. In a heavy saucepan, saute the onion in the oil about 5 minutes until soft.

2. Add the cloves, cinnamon, and coriander. Reduce the heat to medium-low and cook for 1 minute. Stir in the rice and fry until the rice has been well coated with oil.

3. Add the salt and boiling water. Bring the mixture to a boil over medium heat.

4. When the rice begins to boil, cover the pan and reduce the heat to low. Cook the rice for about 15-20 minutes or until all of the water is absorbed and the rice is tender.

5. When the rice is cooked, heat butter in a small skillet and saute the raisins and nuts until they are plump and golden brown.

6. Stir the raisin-nut mixture into the rice and serve.

Gajar Nariyah or Carrots with Grated Coconut *(Serves 12–16)*

Ingredients:

12 large carrots, peeled and cut into thin round slices

1 cup (240 mL) grated coconut

4 teaspoons (20 mL) ground coriander

2 teaspoons (10 mL) ground cumin

1 ¹/₂ cups (360 mL) water

4 teaspoons (20 mL) ground turmeric

10 tablespoons (150 mL) vegetable oil

1 teaspoon (5 mL) mustard seed

¹/₂ cup (120 mL) ground peanuts

Directions:

1. Combine the carrots, coconuts, cumin, coriander, and turmeric in a bowl, mixing well.

2. In a large skillet, saute the mustard seed in the oil until the seeds pop. (Keep a lid handy.)

3. Add the carrot mixture and fry for about 10 minutes. Add water. Lower heat and cook until the carrots are tender, about 10 minutes.

4. Mix the ground peanuts into the cooked carrots and serve.

Girls' Clothing

Sari

The *sari* is the traditional woman's costume in India. It requires 5 yards (4.6 m) of fabric 36-48 (91 cm x 104 cm) inches wide. Buy a length of fabric or split a bed sheet between you and a friend.

Traditionally, women and girls wear a cropped, tight fitting T-shirt and leggings under their sari. Black is most common but any solid colored T-shirt will work. You will also need a wide elastic belt to hold the pleats of the sari in place. Some women use safety pins or small stitches to hold the pleats in place as well.

1. To wrap the sari, take one end of the fabric and tuck it into the waistband at your right hip. Wrap it around your body once. The border of the fabric should just touch the ground (figure A).

2. Make 7 large folds or pleats with the fabric and tuck them into the elastic belt waistband stretching from the right to left hip (figure B).

3. Take the remaining cloth at your left hip and bring it around your back to the front again (figure C).

4. Place the remaining fabric over your left shoulders so that it drapes down your back (figure D).

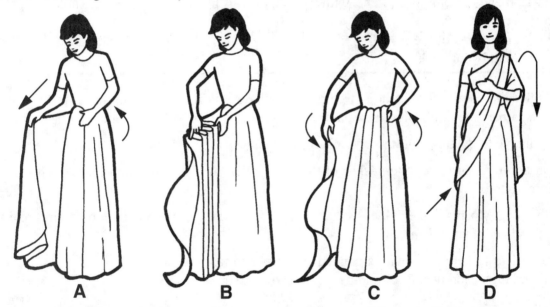

On your feet wear sandals, dance slippers, or espadrilles. Pull your hair back into a bun, wear pigtails, or leave it down. Wear many metal bracelets, anklets, rings, and earrings, as well as necklaces and pendants. On festivals and at weddings, girls decorate their hands and feet with intricate henna patterns. Find examples in books to decorate your hands using non-toxic and non-permanent marker. Some alternatives to the sari are described below.

Alternatives to the Sari:

Wear a long full skirt, tight fitting T-shirt, and a large scarf covering the head

A long scarf may be draped over one shoulder and belted at the waist over a long skirt.

Layer two skirts, one longer than the other. Add a long scarf belted at the waist and draped over the head.

Boys' Clothing

Culottes

In ancient India the most common dress for men included a turban, vest, large cotton collarless shirt, culottes and sandals or slip-on shoes. The culottes will require 2 yards (1.8 m) of fabric 36-48 (91 cm x104 cm) inches wide.

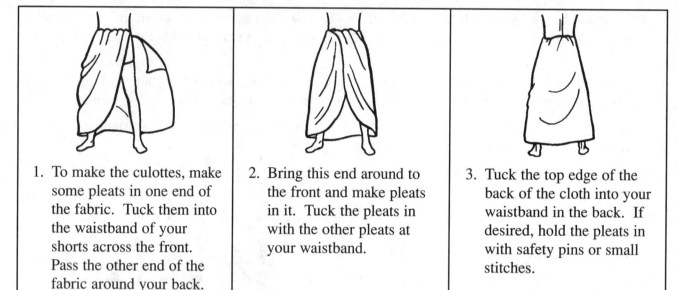

1. To make the culottes, make some pleats in one end of the fabric. Tuck them into the waistband of your shorts across the front. Pass the other end of the fabric around your back.

2. Bring this end around to the front and make pleats in it. Tuck the pleats in with the other pleats at your waistband.

3. Tuck the top edge of the back of the cloth into your waistband in the back. If desired, hold the pleats in with safety pins or small stitches.

Wear a large solid colored T-shirt or a large cotton collarless shirt over the culottes. Add a vest, a turban or head band, and sandals, slippers, or slip-on shoes with jewelry to complete the outfit.

As an alternative to making culottes, try one of these suggestions.

- Wear a long T-shirt over a long skirt of the same color. Add a turban and a wide belt or cummerbund.

- Gather baggy pants at the ankles by tucking them into socks. Top with a long T-shirt and short vest, and add your turban.

- A collarless jacket or one with a banded collar can be worn over narrow pants, a T-shirt, and a cummerbund. Add necklaces and pendants and a turban.

Turban

1. To make a turban, fold two square pieces of cloth or scarves into triangles (figure A).

2. Wrap the first triangle around your head and bring the points to the front. Tie them in a knot with the ends sticking up to form a sort of plume (figure B).

3. Over this, wrap the second triangle (figure C).

4. Tuck two corners of the triangle into the first wrapped cloth, pin the third to the back (figure D).

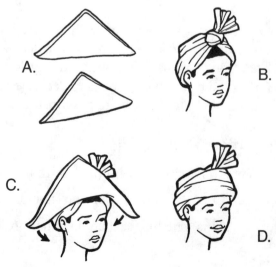

Indian Games

The Waxbill Hunt: Urmila, a princess with a gentle smile, dreamed of owning a waxbill for her bird cage. She promised a tremendous reward to anyone who could fulfill her wish. Soon the best hunters in the country formed bands and set off in hopes of bringing back a small waxbill for the princess.

Play the following game to simulate the waxbill hunt for the princess.

1. Gather 5 large hoops and some chalk.

2. Divide the class into 5 teams and go out onto a large blacktop area.

3. Place one of the hoops on the ground and draw a square with five birds inside as shown.

4. Draw a line about 10 feet (3 meters) from the target to be the throwing line.

5. Line up the teams behind the throwing line and give each team a hoop.

6. Each team takes a turn sending a hunter to the throwing line with the hoop. The hunter throws or rolls the hoop at the target attempting to "capture" as many birds as possible. All of the birds that are completely within the thrown hoop are considered "captured."

7. The first team to capture 20 birds wins the game. If any hunter captures all five birds on one throw, he or she is declared a Master Hunter and receives a special prize.

Guards of the Treasure Room: Maharajah Rampat is known to have a vast treasure in his palace, yet no one has ever seen this treasure, for it is guarded by 10 powerful but blind men. One touch from any of these guards has been said to kill a person instantly. Only the very brave and cunning have ever attempted to steal the Maharajah's treasure! Play the following game to try to steal the treasure.

1. You will need items for the treasure, like strings of beads, plastic pots, etc. The items should be difficult and noisy to carry and too large to be carried in a pocket. Provide 10 blindfolds for the guards.

2. Assign 10 students to be guards and divide the rest of the class into four bandit teams.

3. Place the treasure on the ground in a large open area. Have the guards hold hands and form as large a circle as possible around the treasure. The guards release hands and turn around to face out of the circle.

4. Blindfold the guards and tell them to put their hands on their heads.

5. Outside the circle, about 5 yards (5 meters) away, line up the bandit teams.

6. When the game begins, each team sends one robber to attempt to steal all or part of the treasure. If a guard thinks a robber is near, the guard takes a hand off his or her head to tag the robber. However, guards must remain in place and are only allowed to make one attempt with each hand during the course of the game.

7. If a guard tags a robber, the robber is out of the game and the guard may place both hands back on his or her head for another try. Any piece of treasure held by a robber when he or she is tagged must be returned to the treasure pile.

8. The team with the most treasure is the winning team. If the guards are successful in tagging all robbers, the guards are the winning team.

Ancient India Bulletin Board

Make a large map of India using an opaque projector and the image on page 51. Make seven reference pages using different colors of construction paper to be filled out as you complete the unit. Add pictures from magazines or books to the bulletin board. As art projects are completed, add them to the board as well.

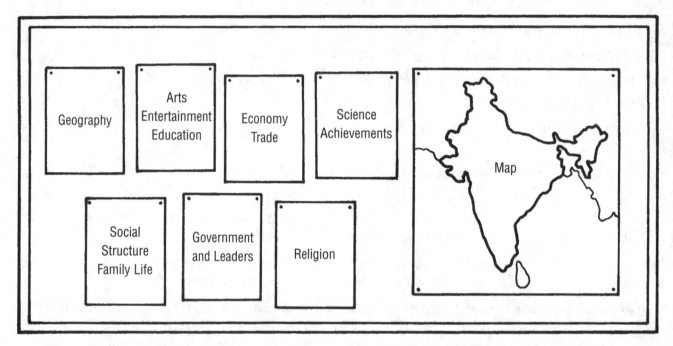

Make a Literature Journal

1. Fold a sheet of construction paper in half for the cover. Have each student decorate the cover with the title of the book, author, and his or her name. Draw an appropriate picture for the cover.

2. Reproduce pages 41 Indian Vocabulary and 51, Make a Map of India for each journal.

3. Assemble the journals by punching holes into the construction paper covers and using brads. This will allow students to add other pages they complete as the unit progresses. Place inside the covers the map, three sheets of blank white paper to make the Physical and Cultural Environment Charts (page 27), the India Vocabulary lists, and ten sheets of writing paper for defining the vocabulary words and taking notes on the various chapters.

4. As you complete each reading selection, have students define words from the vocabulary lists that appeared in their reading. On a separate page, have them write a brief summary of what happened in the section and their thoughts and feelings. Have students write predictions in their journals of what they think will happen in the next reading selection. Check to see if predictions came true.

5. Make sure students are labeling each section in their journals by the chapters covered. As other activities from this unit are completed, punch holes in the pages and add them to the appropriate sections of the journals.

Bibliography and Resources

Nonfiction

Baily, Donna. *India*. Raintree Steck-Vaughn Publishing, 1992.

Braquet, Ann and Martine Noblet. *Tintin's Travel Diaries: India*. Barron's, 1994.

Conkle, Nancy. *A Coloring Book of Ancient India*. Bellerophon Books, 1993.

Ganeri, Anita. *Country Topics for Craft Projects: India*. Watts Books, 1994.

Ganeri, Anita. *What Do We Know: Buddhism*. Peter Bedrick, 1997.

Ganeri, Anita. *What Do We Know: Hinduism*. Peter Bedrick, 1996.

Hermes, Jules. *Children of India*. First Avenue, 1994.

McMair, Sylvia. *Enchantment of the World, India*. Children's Press, 1990.

National Geographic. Volume 191, Number 5, May 1997.

Neurath, Marie and John Ellis. *They Lived Like This in Ancient India*. Franklin Watts, 1967.

Roth, Susan L. *Buddha*. Doubleday, 1994.

Srinivasan, Radhika. *Cultures of the World, India*. Marshall Cavendish, 1990.

Wirsing, Robert and Nancy. *Ancient India*. Franklin Watts, 1973.

Fiction

Alexander, Lloyd. *Iron Ring*. Dutton's Childrens Books, 1997.

Barry, D. *The Rajah's Rice: A Mathematical Folktale from India*. W.H. Freeman & Co., 1994.

Bond, Ruskin. *Binya's Blue Umbrella*. Boyds Mill Press, 1995.

Dalal-Clayton, Diksha. *The Adventures of Young Krishna: The Blue God of India*. Oxford Press, 1992.

Godden, Rumer. *Premlata and The Festival of Light*. Greenwillow Press, 1997.

Haviland, Virginia. *Favorite Fairy Tales Told in India*. Little Brown & Company, 1973.

Highwater, Jamake. *Rama: A Legend*. Henry Holt and Co., 1994.

Hirsh, Marilyn. *The Elephants and the Mice*. The World Publishing Company, 1970.

Husain, Shahrukh. *Demons, Gods, & Holy Men from Indian Myths and Legends*. Peter Bedrick Books, 1987.

Jaffrey, Madhur and Michael Foreman. *Seasons of Splendor: Myths and Legends of India*. Viking, 1992.

Rana, Indi. *Roller Birds of Rampur*. Henry Holt, 1993.

Rose, D.L. *The People Who Hugged Trees*. Roberts, Rinehart, Inc., 1990.

Videos

Gandhi. Columbia Pictures Industries, 1982.

India, Land of Spirit and Mystique. International Video Network, 1988.

Jungle Book. The Walt Disney Video, 1995.

Mahabharata. The Parabola Video Library, 1989.

Tiger and the Brahman. The Rabbit Ears Production, 1991.

Computer Programs

Cryptoquest, Dueling Digits, Museum Madness, Sky Lab, Time Navigator Around the World, all from MECC

On Line Resources

www.geocities.com/Tokyo/5215 (Buddha and Sanskrit links)

www.cs.colostate.edu/~malaiya/jainhout/html (outline of ancient Indian beliefs with many links)

Key for Page 51

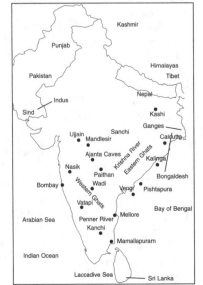

Answer Key

Page 9

1. **Aryans:** *Highest:* Brahmans, scholars and priests; *Upper:* Kshatriyas, kings and warriors; *Middle:* Vaishyas, merchants and farmers; *Lower:* Sudras, peasants and servants; *Outcasts:* Panchamas. **Our Society:** Accept reasonable answers.
2. Aryans were born into their class. They performed specific jobs based on their class, wore special clothes, cords, and hairstyles.
3. Accept reasonable answers.
4. Most likely the Aryans considered themselves superior to the native people.
5. Hitler used the term to specify a certain race of people as superior to all others in the world. He felt it gave him the right to kill people whom he did not consider Aryan.

Page 12

1. Both believe in reincarnation, karma, and leading an honorable life without harming others. Hinduism bases reincarnation and karma on caste; Buddhism does not. Hindus worship many gods, yet Buddhism presents no gods.
2. If people were satisfied with Hindu beliefs, a new religion would not attract many people.
3. The people who did convert to Buddhism were unhappy with their social and spiritual positions in Hinduism. Buddhism offered them equality and hope of reaching fulfillment.
4. The upper classes did not convert to Buddhism because they would lose status and power in the community. They fought the new religion because it undermined their power.
5. Answers may vary.
6. Answers may vary.

Page 31

Chapter 5 1. An elephant has poor eyesight but a keen sense of smell and touch. He senses vibrations through his legs and uses his trunk like a hand. 2. He eats six times the weight of a man. 3. An elephant's skin can burn in the sun and tears easily. 4. He can run fast but cannot jump. When he walks he sways back and forth. 5. An elephant is very loyal to a good master but will destroy a bad one.
Chapter 6 1. When elephants meet they sniff with extended trunks, tip to tip, and sometimes they thrust their trunks into each other's mouths. 2. They use different sounds—grunting, roaring, barking, rumbling, and even whistling; anger is expressed by snorting loudly and smacking a trunk against a tree; to express sickness it grumbles deep in its throat; to express surprise it squeals like a human child; squeaking means pleasure; purring means contentment; trumpeting frightens other animals. 3. The higher an elephant holds its head, the more excited it is. 4. Elephants swim under water using their trunks like snorkels. 5. A good mahout uses his toes to nudge the elephant at the base of the ear.
Chapter 7 1. A keddah 2. Elephants are slow going down a hill. 3. Men beat pieces of metal and the elephants try to escape the noise. They followed their leader, herded by the men and the noise, to the corral entrance.
Chapter 8 1. Tame, well-trained female elephants used to control newly captured elephants. 2. Selected elephants are led out of the keddah with a koomkie on each side and tied to a tree. The elephant is then transferred into a "crush" or cage of timber. 3. They can smell fear. 4. One must beat to train the animal, not to hurt him. 5. When an elephant tries to shake the handler off his back.
Chapter 9 1. He rolls over on his side and gives a great sigh. 2. He is the four-tusked white elephant ridden by the god Indra. 3. The mahout repeats, "I am a mahout loyal to my king—I belong to my gaja—I serve my king by living for my gaja." Then he is given an ankus.

Page 38

1. He thinks he will become famous for fighting and news will spread about him and his search for his sister. 2. The clothes will make him more visible and draw more attention to him in battle, causing more fame. 3. Accept reasonable answers. 4. They think he has become vain and foolish with his new clothes—a glory fighter. 5. Vasu finally attacks him during a battle, knocking him off of Gandiva. 6. Gandiva was his one true friend, and now he is all alone again. 7 and 8. Accept reasonable answers.

Page 39

Rama: friend, wise mahout mentor who taught duty and loyalty
Gandiva: friend, elephant who taught friendship and loyalty; gave comfort
Skanda: foe, mahout who mishandled his gaja and was killed; taught Arjun about honesty and bad karma
Hari: friend, fellow mahout who taught friendship and loyalty
Vasu: foe, Arjun's envious sergeant; taught Arjun to be careful whom he angered and to consider threats as real
Manoja: friend, old man in prison camp who was like a charming, unreliable older brother; taught Arjun confidence and hope

Page 51 See page 79

Page 54

1. They came for the rich soil and other resources. 2. Oven baked bricks were strong enough to withstand the flood waters. They may have used up the fuel supply by cutting down all of the trees to use in firing the bricks. 3. Cities far from each other were planned in the same basic layout and used the same basic items. There were few changes in artifacts over 1,000 years. 4. They had advanced sewage and organized city planning that required cooperation of many people working together. 5. hairstyles, jewelry, cotton cloth, chicken raising, stand-up baths, toys, public baths, and god images. 6. Accept reasonable answers.

Page 56–58

1. Agni	7. Ganga
2. Ganesha	8. Vishnu
3. Brahma	9. Durga
4. Krishna	10. Surya
5. Shiva	11. Parvati
6. Indra	

Page 60

1. Tyre, Athens
2. Athens, Rome, Carthage

 ©Teacher Created Materials, Inc.